As one of the world's longest established
and best-known travel brands,
Thomas Cook are the experts in travel.

For more than 135 years our
guidebooks have unlocked the secrets
of destinations around the world,
sharing with travellers a wealth of
experience and a passion for travel.

**Rely on Thomas Cook as your
travelling companion on your next trip
and benefit from our unique heritage.**

Thomas Cook **traveller** guides

LANGUEDOC-
ROUSSILLON

Robin Gauldie

Written by Robin Gauldie
Original photography by Robin Gauldie and Johanne Clyne

Published by Thomas Cook Publishing
A division of Thomas Cook Tour Operations Limited
Company registration no. 3772199 England
The Thomas Cook Business Park, Unit 9, Coningsby Road,
Peterborough PE3 8SB, United Kingdom
Email: books@thomascook.com, Tel: +44 (0) 1733 416477
www.thomascookpublishing.com

Produced by Cambridge Publishing Management Limited
Burr Elm Court, Main Street, Caldecote CB23 7NU
www.cambridgepm.co.uk

ISBN: 978-1-84848-472-6

First edition © 2011 Thomas Cook Publishing
Text © Thomas Cook Publishing
Maps © Thomas Cook Publishing/PCGraphics (UK) Limited
Transport map © Communicarta Limited

Series Editor: Karen Beaulah
Production/DTP: Steven Collins

Printed and bound in Spain by GraphyCems

Cover photography © I CAPTURE PHOTOGRAPHY/Alamy

Contents

Introduction

Between the soaring peaks of the Pyrénées and the thickly wooded valleys of the Lozère and the Massif Central to the north, with the Mediterranean lapping its sunny, sandy east coast, Languedoc-Roussillon is a region that until quite recently was overlooked by foreign visitors. Yet it's one of the most attractive parts of France, with a mellow climate, a fascinating history, an amazing variety of scenery, tiny villages and bustling market towns, and lively university cities.

And the food and drink here will satisfy even the most demanding gourmand. Long overshadowed by its more glamorous (and gastronomically renowned) neighbour, Provence (as well as by the Dordogne, France's 'Little England', to the northwest), Languedoc came of age, tourism-wise, in the 1990s, with the opening up of low-cost flights to half a dozen airports in and around the region, and with the completion of France's latest high-speed rail links.

The mini-boom that followed was clearly long overdue. This is a region that offers a wider choice of holiday experiences than almost anywhere else in France, or indeed in Europe. It's a part of France that is just as attractive for a short getaway as for a longer holiday. For a long weekend or a midweek break, Carcassonne, Perpignan, Montpellier and Nîmes have plenty to offer, while for a fortnight's holiday it's easy to combine an idle week in the sun with a week's touring, walking, riding or cycling. Visitors can

mingle with the locals on market day or in a village café, visit ancient caves, medieval abbeys and castles or gleaming new museums and art galleries, or just laze in the sun by a villa pool, a mountain lake or a Mediterranean beach.

The choice of holiday sporting activities is equally wide. The long, wide beaches of the Mediterranean coast are perfect for wind- and watersports such as windsurfing and kite-boarding, sailing and sand-yachting, and there is excellent scuba diving off the rocky coast near Collioure and Banyuls, near the Spanish border.

Inland, there's scenery that is perfect for a gentle stroll or for a demanding long-distance mountain hike or bike trip, while the region's waterways offer everything from easy-going canal cruising to white-water rafting and kayaking – and all of this is within delightfully easy reach of Languedoc's main gateway points and holiday resorts.

On the Mediterranean coast, these resorts include some of France's better-known, purpose-built holiday locations, ranging from the futuristic, pyramid-style apartment complexes of La Grande-Motte to the 'textile-free' naturist summer city of Le Cap d'Agde. And the choice of places to stay across the region is dazzlingly diverse, whether you are interested in charming *pensions* and *chambres d'hôtes* in smaller towns and villages, countryside *gîtes* and villas with pools, campsites by the sea and in the hills, or a portfolio of some outstanding small, intimate luxury hotels.

Languedoc, too, is a joy for those in search of culture and heritage. The region is studded with relics from every human era, so you'll find caves once used by prehistoric people, ancient Celtic dolmens, Roman theatres, pinnacle-perched Cathar castles and medieval cathedrals.

Attractive floral decorations adorn many homes

The land

The modern French region of Languedoc-Roussillon is the result of a merging of two much older entities. Languedoc – the larger of the two – stretches from the garrigue-covered hillsides of the Corbières to the thickly wooded slopes of the Montagne Noire and the Cévennes, embracing the fertile plains of the Aude valley and the vineyards of the Hérault and the Minervois, with the Rhône delta on its eastern edge.

Roussillon, to the south, occupies a wide swathe of Pyrenean foothills, valleys and dizzying mountain summits stretching from the Ariège in the west all the way to the Mediterranean coast, and bounded to the south by France's border with Spain.

Climate

The region's climate is influenced by the Atlantic, the Mediterranean, and the mountain ranges of the Pyrénées and the Massif Central. The east wind known as 'la Grecque' brings clear blue skies and hot weather in summer, while west winds from the Atlantic can bring cooler weather and outbreaks of heavy rain. In winter, the south wind called the 'Tramontane', blowing down from the snowy peaks of the Pyrénées, brings the coldest weather.

Summers are long and usually sunny, though heavy thunderstorms are not uncommon, especially in the high country of Haut-Languedoc. Summer temperatures can rise to 35°C (95°F) and higher. Autumn weather is mellower and rain is more frequent, but daytime temperatures can rise to above 20°C (68°F) even in early November. Winters are short but sharp, with heavy snow on higher ground and occasional spells of sub-zero daytime temperatures even in the lowlands between December and February.

The *départements*

Each of the five *départements* of the Languedoc-Roussillon region has its own distinct character, geography and even climate. The Aude and Hérault areas are the gentlest, most fertile and least rugged (though each includes areas of mountain and forest). The region's most awe-inspiring mountain landscapes are on its southern fringe, where the high peaks of the Pyrénées-Orientales form a natural barrier between France and the Iberian Peninsula. Not quite as high, but equally rugged, are the highlands and deep river gorges of Languedoc's two

An antique farm cart provides a glimpse into the region's agricultural past

less-populated northern sub-divisions, the Gard and the Lozère.

Mountains, rivers and wetlands

The hills and mountains of Languedoc are formed mainly of porous limestone, and so despite heavy winter rains and snows they are arid for much of the year, creating the typical *garrigue* ecosystem of scrubland that dominates much of the eastern part of the region. To the south, the Pyrénées rise to their highest point at the Pic du Canigou, 2,785m (9,137ft) above sea level; the higher slopes are treeless, with only a few hardy shrubs clinging in sheltered spots, but the lower slopes of the Pyrénées are heavily wooded with holm oak and conifers. To the north, granite geology creates a greener ecosystem, with thick forests covering the Montagne Noire hills, north of Carcassonne, and the uplands of the Haut-Languedoc.

Between these two mountainous areas lies the valley of the Aude, Languedoc's major waterway, which flows from the Pyrénées southwards to Carcassonne, then eastward to the sea. Over millennia, the river has created a wide and fertile floodplain that for centuries has been one of France's highest-volume winegrowing areas. The Hérault, flowing south from its source in the Cévennes, irrigates another vineyard-filled valley, while the Gard and the Petit-Rhône rivers together define the eastern boundary of Languedoc.

Shared with neighbouring Provence, the Camargue region is a unique area of wetlands formed by the wide delta of the Rhône, while broad, shallow lagoons called *étangs* are a typical feature of the Mediterranean coast.

Wildlife

Languedoc's wide variety of ecosystems fosters a fascinating array of wildlife. The distinctive call of the cuckoo and the drumming of woodpeckers are typical early summer sounds in woodland areas, while the screaming of high-flying swifts is ever present in the evenings during high summer. Flamingos, egrets and many other migrant bird species frequent the coastal wetlands, and raptors such as golden eagles, buzzards and griffon vultures can be seen in the mountains of the Cévennes and the Pyrénées. The Pyrénées are also home to the shy *izard* (Pyrenean chamois). *Sanglier* (wild boar) and *chevreuil* (roe deer) are numerous, despite being

The scenic limestone landscape near Minerve

enthusiastically hunted, and are often seen crossing rural roads. Insect life is profuse, and includes some outstandingly beautiful butterflies, such as the scarce swallowtail with its black-and-white zebra stripes, and the even more spectacular purple emperor. Equally striking are the night-flying moths of the region. Blue- and red-winged grasshoppers leap from underfoot on hill paths, and other fascinating critters include the praying mantis, with its eerily human posture, bulging eyes and clawed forearms designed to trap its insect prey. You will meet several species of wall lizard in rocky countryside and on village walls, see big green lizards scuttling across roads and paths, and you're also likely to hear the croaking of green tree frogs and edible frogs in wetland areas in the evenings, and encounter black-and-yellow salamanders in forest streams and pools.

Languedoc's unique wildlife is protected in a number of parks and nature reserves, including the vast Parc Naturel Régional du Haut-Languedoc (Regional Nature Park of Haut-Languedoc) and Parc National des Cévennes (National Park of the Cévennes) in the northern hills, the Parc Naturel Régional des Pyrénées Catalanes (Regional Nature Park of the Catalan Pyrénées) on the Spanish border and, on the fringes of the Camargue wetlands, the Parc Naturel Régional de Camargue (Regional Nature Park of the Camargue).

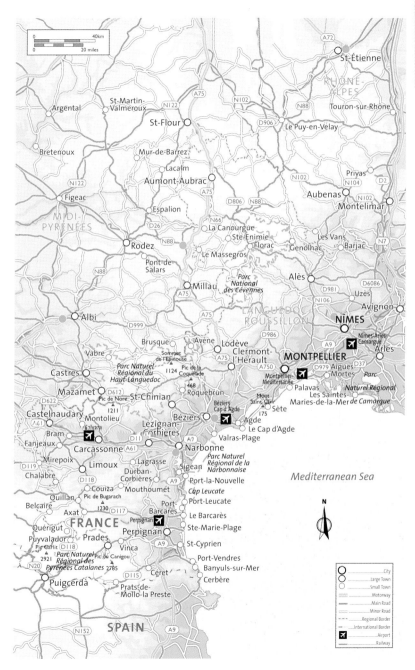

History

c. **500,000** BC	Early humans live as hunter-gatherers.
c. **150,000–35,000** BC	Neanderthals inhabit the Aude valley and the foothills of the Pyrénées.
c. **12,000** BC	First true humans (*Homo sapiens*) occupy the area.
c. **800** BC	Bronze-working Celts build fortified settlements on hilltops, while Phoenicians and Greeks establish coastal trading posts.
3rd century BC	Roman occupation begins. Via Domitia is built, linking Roman Narbo (later called Narbonne) with Rome and Spain.
27 BC	Narbo becomes capital of the new Roman province, Septimania.
5th–6th century	Visigoths take control of Septimania.
Early 8th century	Muslims from North Africa ('Moors') conquer Spain and southern France. They are driven back over the Pyrénées by Charlemagne; Languedoc becomes part of the Christian Frankish kingdom.
8th–10th century	Occitan, or the 'Langue d'Oc' becomes the main language of the region.
10th century	Languedoc is ruled by the Counts of Toulouse. Roussillon becomes part of the county of the 'Spanish March'. Maguelone (later called Montpellier) is founded.
1208	Pope Innocent III proclaims the Albigensian Crusade against the heretical Cathars. Crusaders led by Simon de Montfort take Carcassonne and capture Count Raymond VI.
1218	Count Raymond VI returns Languedoc to Catholicism.
1220s	Louis XIII and Louis IX overthrow Raymond VI to make Languedoc part of France, but Roussillon remains part of the Catalan kingdom of Majorca.

1242–6	The last Cathar strongholds at Montségur, Puilaurens and Quéribus are besieged and captured.
1337–1453	Hundred Years War. Much of Languedoc is pillaged by English troops. 'Black Death' (The Plague) kills many. The English are driven out after defeat at Castillon.
16th century	Many local people become Huguenot (French Protestant) converts.
1659	Spain recognises French control of Roussillon.
1666	The Canal du Midi, between Toulouse and Agde, is completed.
18th century	Widespread hunger and discontent culminate in revolution, the declaration of the Republic (1792) and the execution of Louis XVI (1793).
1793–1815	Revolutionary and Napoleonic Wars. France is defeated after more than 20 years of warfare.
19th century	Montpellier and other cities develop into industrial centres.

	Phylloxera plague (1875) ruins the region's vineyards.
1914–18	World War 1. Thousands of local men die in the trenches of northern France.
1940	France defeated by Germany in World War II.
1942–4	Southern France occupied by Germany. French Resistance fighters (*résistants*) operate from the Cévennes, the Pyrénées and Haut-Languedoc. In retaliation, Germans murder many civilians. Germans withdraw in June 1944.
1958	France is founder member of the European Common Market (forerunner of the European Union).
1977	Construction of new Antigone district begins in Montpellier.
2008	Winegrowers riot in Montpellier.
2014–16	Main sections of the high-speed train link between Nîmes and Barcelona are due for completion.

Politics

Languedoc-Roussillon is one of the 26 regions which comprise metropolitan France. The region is made up of five départements (administrative districts): Aude, Hérault, Gard, Lozère and the Pyrénées-Orientales. Embracing one of France's larger cities as well as several large provincial towns, it also comprises large areas of thinly populated countryside, dotted with tiny villages and small family-owned farms, as well as huge vineyards and equally large stretches of intensive agro-industrial farming.

Languedoc-Roussillon has a total area of 27,376sq km (10,570sq miles) and a population of 2,589,704 (2008 census). The population grew by 12.7 per cent between 1999 and 2008, reversing a decades-long decline, partly as a result of immigration from former French colonies and from other EU countries, and partly because economic renewal in cities such as Montpellier has attracted people back to the region.

Population density is still low, even by French standards, with around 84 people per square kilometre (compared with a national average of 109) and even lower in comparison with England's 395 people per square kilometre – a factor that has attracted thousands of English people to Languedoc. Montpellier, the regional capital, is also the region's biggest city. With a population of around 254,976 (2008 census), it has grown rapidly: in 1980 it was France's 25th-largest city, and it is now the 8th largest.

Languedoc's other major towns and cities are Nîmes (population 147,114), Perpignan (117,500), Béziers (74,028), Narbonne (51,956) and Carcassonne (48,212). More than a third of the population live in the towns and cities of the Mediterranean coast and the Aude valley, leaving broad swathes of forested uplands that are almost uninhabited, with just a scattering of little villages and hamlets in highland areas such as the Cerdagne (next to Spain), the Cévennes, the Montagne Noire and Haut-Languedoc.

All of this creates political tensions between the needs and ambitions of town and city folk, large agro-industrial concerns, small farmers and winegrowers (some of whom rioted in Montpellier in 2008, demanding government aid to offset rising costs and falling prices for their product). Keeping these varied constituencies happy involves local politicians in a never-ending juggling act as they attempt to satisfy voters while at the same time answering to the national government in Paris, which ultimately holds the purse strings.

Elections are due in 2012 for the French National Assembly, to which Languedoc sends 21 deputies. At the 2007 elections, the centre-right Union pour un Mouvement Populaire (UMP, Union for a Popular Movement) won 19 seats, the Parti Socialist (PS, Socialist Party) won 11, with two small independent parties taking the remaining two.

Historically, Languedoc-Roussillon has leaned to the left, and many streets are named after the locally born leftist politician Jean Jaurès (1859–1914) whose statue stands in a number of town squares.

The president of the Regional Assembly from 2004 until his death in October 2010 was Georges Frêche, a former Socialist Party leader who was ejected from the party in 2007 after a series of allegedly racist speeches. Race, religion and immigration remain difficult issues in the region, where many people are of North African descent, while others are more recent arrivals from France's former African colonies. Despite his controversial style and leftist sympathies, Frêche, who was previously mayor of Montpellier, left quite a legacy by leading an administration that encouraged investment in the city and the region, attracting new industries and developing the city as a centre of scientific and technological expertise.

Politics

Georges Frêche in conversation with officials of a local rugby team in March 2010

Regional specialities

With its tremendous variety of landscapes and microclimates, Languedoc-Roussillon produces a mouth-wateringly wide menu of regional and local specialities, from wild fungi and game from the hills and forests, to plump shellfish from the coastal lagoons, beef from the lush pastures of the Camargue and lamb from the hills of Cabardès and the Lozère.

The emphasis throughout the region is on uncomplicated, hearty food, simply prepared and often uncompromisingly rich and filling. In the Aude, the signature dish is *cassoulet*, a stew of white beans, sausage, duck, pork and goose fat. Castelnaudary, on the Canal du Midi, is the acknowledged capital of this artery-clogging snack. *Confit de canard* (duck preserved in its own fat) is another calorie-rich favourite. Wild

Fresh herbs and spices at a local market

boar (*sanglier*) appears on the menu during the autumn and winter hunting season, and there's no need to feel guilty about tucking in: boar are as common as ever. Local *charcutiers* take pride in using virtually all of the animal, with choice cuts being roasted or casseroled while the rest becomes sausage, *terrine* or *rillettes* (similar to pâté).

The same woods that shelter the *sanglier* also yield a bounty of *cèpes*, *porquerolles*, *chanterelles*, *trompettes de mort* and other wild fungi in autumn, and Uzès, north of Nîmes, is famous for truffles. Freshly picked fungi can be found in the region's markets in September and October, and dried varieties are sold year-round. The vineyards of the Aude and the Hérault traditionally yield crops of plump and tasty Roman snails (*escargots*), which are cooked and flavoured with garlic – preferably the pungent and much-prized pink garlic of Haut-Languedoc.

The high country of the Cévennes, the Hérault, the Corbières and the Cabardès is prime grazing country for sheep and goats, and produces a great variety of distinctive cheeses made from their milk, such as the creamy, nutty-tasting Pélardon. Bleu des Causses and

Mediterranean seafood is readily available

Tome are typical cheeses of the Lozère region. Céret, in the eastern Pyrenean foothills, is famous for its cherries, Nîmes for its strawberries, and the Cévennes for its chestnuts.

Beekeeping is popular, and honey comes in dozens of distinctive flavours, each influenced by the flowering shrubs, plants and trees closest to the hives. Chestnut honey from the Cévennes, Montagne Noire, and Olargues in the Hérault is renowned for its nutty taste, while aromatic herbs such as thyme and oregano lend a unique aroma to honey from hives region-wide.

The wetlands of the Camargue are famed for their many varieties of rice, used in paella, risotto and to accompany fish and meat dishes, as well as for the rich meat of the *taureau Camarguais*, the black cattle which graze the Camargue's lush pastures.

Heading down the coast, the Sète fishing fleet brings in a rich haul of Mediterreanean seafood, some of which goes into the renowned local fish stew, *bourride* (similar to the Provençal *bouillabaisse*). Oysters are farmed in the shallow waters of the Étang de Thau and other coastal lagoons, which also produce delicious clams, mussels, cockles and other shellfish, and down near the Spanish border the deep waters off Collioure yield a rich catch of anchovies, sardines and other blue-water fish.

The region is better known for delivering vast quantities of cheap and cheerful *vins de table* than for great wines, but it does boast a few notable *appellations*, including Blanquette de Limoux, which claims to be the world's first sparkling wine, and the unique *vins gris de sables*, made from grapes grown in the sandy soil of the Camargue. You'll also encounter spirits (*eaux de vie*) flavoured with all sorts of fruit and nuts, including peach, cherry and walnut.

Culture

The region's cultural roots reach deep into the 12th and 13th centuries, when the troubadours who played and sang at the noble courts of the Langue d'Oc were famed throughout Christendom for their ballads of passion, romance and courtly love. Love of music and dance is still very much part of life in Languedoc, especially in summer, when the region hosts hundreds of open-air events.

These events constitute everything from world-class music, dance and drama festivals in Carcassonne and Montpellier to one-night parties in village squares. Performance spaces range from historic buildings such as Carcassonne's glorious 17th-century Baroque Collège des Jésuites, which was restored in the 2000s and is now the venue for the city's annual jazz festival, to Montpellier's grandiose Opéra Comédie, home to the Opéra Orchestre National de Montpellier Languedoc-Roussillon.

There's a movement to revive the distinctive Occitan dialect as a literary, sung and spoken tongue, on a par with Catalan, which also has a cultural claim on the region. Many public buildings in the southeast part of the region, near the Spanish border, fly the red and yellow colours of Catalunya (Catalonia) alongside the French *drapeau tricolore* (tricolour), and roadsigns often display the original Catalan or Occitan place name as well as the modern French

version – Perpignan, for example, is also called Perpinyà.

Age-old folkore survives, too. The Catalan *sardana* or *sardane* is danced at many festivals in Perpignan and around the Pyrénées-Orientales. Since 1955, when the ancient tradition was revived, thousands of people gather each Midsummer's Eve for a huge bonfire atop the Pic du Canigou, from where blazing torches are carried by runners to Perpignan and other towns and villages on both sides of the border. The *Fête de l'Ours* (Bear Festival) at Prat de Mollo, when pelt-clad 'bears' are chased through the streets by axe-wielding 'hunters', must surely have survived from pre-Christian times, like the legend of the fearsome river-monster, the *tarasque*.

While Occitan and Catalan traditions still influence the area, the Camargue region proudly retains its own distinctive culture. It is a major centre for the travelling *Gitan* or Rom communities of France and Spain, who

A Catalan flavour shows in the celebrations of a local rugby triumph in Perpignan

gather at Les Saintes-Maries-de-la-Mer in May and October for two great horse-trading fairs, where they mingle with the black-clad *gardians* who raise the Camargue's famous fighting bulls and black cattle.

Languedoc-Roussillon has an astonishing architectural patrimony. UNESCO World Heritage Sites include the walled medieval city of Carcassonne, the Roman relics of Nîmes and the Pont du Gard, the Romanesque-Baroque Cathédrale Saint-Nazaire in Béziers, and a profusion of Romanesque village churches. More recently, it has also produced cutting-edge architecture

such as the daring Antigone Quarter of Montpellier, designed by the Catalan architect Ricardo Bofill and inspired by the Roman architecture of Nîmes.

Historically, Languedoc-Roussillon has offered a haven to painters, including Pablo Picasso, Georges Braque, Henri Matisse, Modigliani and many others. All of them made their way in the early 20th century to the little village of Céret, close to the Spanish border, where Picasso lived for some time and where an excellent museum exhibits a selection of his work, along with paintings, prints and sculptures by a number of artists of the Fauvist movement.

Festivals and events

Languedoc loves a good party and the region plays host to a calendar of events great and small, from high-profile festivals attracting some of the world's greatest performers to fun local events that are the high point of summer in smaller towns and villages. Venues can be state-of-the-art city concert halls and stadiums, Nîmes' ancient Roman theatre, village squares, or floodlit medieval castles.

Festivals and events take place year-round, but July is the busiest month for star performances.

Mid-January–March
Carnaval
Limoux claims its three-month festival is the longest carnival in the world, with musical performances under the arcades of the town square every weekend, culminating in the ceremonial effigy cremation of Sa Majesté Carnaval (Carnival King).
Place de la République, Limoux. Tel: (0468) 31 01 16. www.limoux.fr. Free admission.

April
Carcassonne Jazz Week
Four days of modern and classic jazz by French and international artists in the grand restored Baroque chapel.
Chapelle de la Collège des Jésuites, Carcassonne. Tel: (0468) 10 24 30. www.carcassonne.org. Admission charge.

Mid-June–mid-August
Festival de Carcassonne
The Carcassonne Festival is the cultural high point of summer in Languedoc, with more than 100 performances (most of them free) spanning hard rock, jazz, theatre, dance and circus, and high-profile artists such as (in 2010) Bob Dylan, Jamiroquai, Simple Minds, Motorhead and Suzanne Vega.
Various venues, Carcassonne. Tel: (0468) 11 59 15. www.carcassonne.org. Admission charge for some performances.

June–July
Montpellier Danse
Launched in 1980, this event has become one of Europe's leading dance festivals, attracting hundreds of dance companies and some of the world's leading choreographers.
Various venues, Montpellier. Tel: (0467) 60 83 60. www.montpellierdanse.com. Admission charge.

July

Fêtes de Saint-Pierre

A solemn procession to commemorate those lost at sea as well as traditional 'water-jousting' contests.
Sète. Tel: (0499) 04 71 71.
www.ot-sete.fr. Free admission.

14 July (Bastille Day)

France's major national festival celebrates the Revolution and the rebirth of France with military parades, music, and spectacular fireworks.
Various venues. www.sunfrance.com.
Admission charge for some events.

Les Estivales de Perpignan

More than 600 performers gather in Perpignan for a month of open-air song, dance and comedy.
Le Campo Santo, Place Gambetta, Perpignan. Tel: 0892 68 36 22.
www.estivales.com. Admission charge.

Festival de Radio France

Three weeks of symphonic music, opera, jazz, world music and reggae.
Various venues, Montpellier.
Tel: (0467) 02 02 01.
www.festivalradiofrancemontpellier.com.
Admission charge for some performances.

Les Nuits Musicales d'Uzès

From mid-July to the end of July, the picturesque town of Uzès hosts a programme of classical music.
Place de l'Évêché, Uzès.
Tel: (0466) 62 20 00. www.nuits musicalesuzes.org. Admission charge.

Festival de Nîmes

A spectacular week of rock and pop from international legends and newcomers in the city's Roman arena.

The annual visit of the Tour de France

Arènes de Nîmes, 4 boulevard des Arènes. Tel: (0467) 92 23 53.
www.festivaldenimes.com. Admission charge for some performances.

Le Tour de France

Several stages pass through Languedoc, although routings change annually.
www.letour.fr. Free admission.

August

Spectacle Médiéval

Dramatic knightly combats, jugglers, troubadours and acrobats enliven Carcassonne's medieval city for two days in mid-August.
La Cité & La Bastide de Saint-Louis, Carcassonne. Tel: (0468) 10 24 30.
www.carcassonne.org. Free admission for most events.

October

Les Primeurs d'Oc

The region's biggest wine festival, held in early October.
Béziers. www.beziers-tourisme.fr.
Admission charge for some events.

Highlights

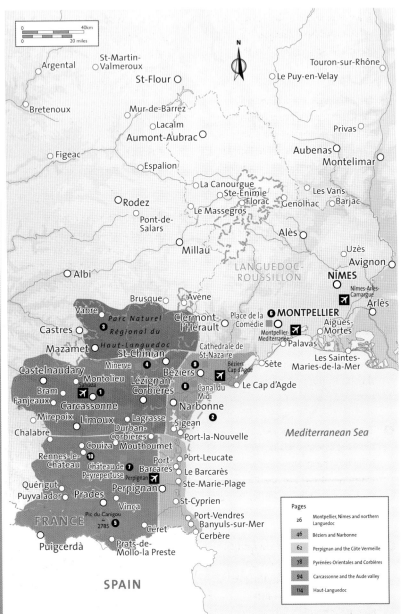

Pages	
26	Montpellier, Nîmes and northern Languedoc
46	Béziers and Narbonne
62	Perpignan and the Côte Vermeille
78	Pyrénées-Orientales and Corbières
94	Carcassonne and the Aude valley
114	Haut-Languedoc

❶ Walking round the massive medieval ramparts and turrets of **Carcassonne**, the signature sight of the Aude and Languedoc, painstakingly restored in the 19th century.

❷ **Swimming**, sunbathing, surfboarding or beachcombing among the dunes, breezy strands favoured by windsurfers, family-friendly beaches with lifeguards or 'textile-free' resorts.

❸ Walking the **Grandes Randonnées** mountain and forest trails of the Parc Naturel Régional du Haut-Languedoc, the most accessible and rewarding of the region's park areas.

❹ Strolling through the cobbled streets of **Minerve**, perched high above the plains and vineyards of the Aude, a postcard-pretty village with a dramatic past.

❺ Taking in the breathtaking views of France, Spain, the Mediterranean and the Pyrénées from the summit of the **Pic du Canigou**, 2,785m (9,137ft) above sea level.

❻ Lazing and watching the world go by from a café terrace on Montpellier's bustling **Place de la Comédie**, the hub of the regional capital.

❼ Making the dizzy ascent to the ramparts of the **Château de Peyrepertuse**, the most spectacular of the many Cathar castles, and wondering how its besiegers ever managed to capture this seemingly impregnable cliff-top stronghold.

❽ Floating gently along the **Canal du Midi** on a live-aboard narrowboat, pausing for lunch, dinner and drinks at canalside villages along the way.

❾ Admiring the Romanesque-Baroque interior of the 13th-century **Cathédrale Saint-Nazaire** in Béziers, the region's most impressive place of worship.

❿ Untangling the hidden mysteries of the chapel of Mary Magdalene at **Rennes-le-Château**, the inspiration for Dan Brown's blockbuster *The Da Vinci Code*.

The medieval Porte D'Aude in Carcassonne

Suggested itineraries

Long weekend:
around Carcassonne

There are few better places than
Carcassonne for a two- or three-night
break. You won't need a car for this short
itinerary, as the city is easier to explore on
foot and the old fortified part of town is
almost entirely car-free. The railway
station is just outside the centre of the
lower town and the airport is only
minutes away. In summer a handy tourist
navette shuttles between Place Carnot in
the centre of the Bastide de Saint-Louis
(also known as the Ville Basse), the
slightly more modern part of town, and
the medieval Cité. On a hot summer day
this is a welcome alternative to walking
up the steep streets that lead to the city.

Day 1

Starting at the massive gateway of
the Porte d'Aude, walk around the
impressive ramparts and bastions of the
Cité, taking time for a guided tour
(approximately 45 minutes) of the 12th-
century Château Comtal, the stronghold
of the Counts of Trencavel. Don't miss
the Basilica of Saint-Nazaire, with its
leering gargoyles, and for a different
experience visit Les Oiseaux de la Cité,
where hawks, falcons and eagles put on
a striking display in summer.

Day 2

Explore the quaintly evocative streets of
the Ville Basse, browse through the
morning market on Place Carnot

(which sells everything from fresh fruit
and vegetables to live ducklings, day-
old chicks and baby rabbits), sip an
apéritif at a pavement café, visit the
Musée des Beaux-Arts and enjoy a
leisurely dinner at one of the town's
good restaurants (with a couple of
pricey exceptions, you'll eat better
among the locals in the Ville Basse than
among fellow tourists in the restaurants
of the Cité).

Day 3

Spend the day exploring the striking
hilltop Cathar castles of Lastours
(15km/9 miles north of Carcassonne)
either independently or on an escorted
day trip, then stay on for a lively
medieval banquet and a spectacular *Son
et luminièr* (sound and light) show.

One week: the Mediterranean
coast

You can explore the full length of the
Mediterranean coast using public
transport (a combination of train and
bus), starting in Nîmes and returning
by train or plane from Perpignan (or
the other way round). Nîmes and
Montpellier each merit a busy day's
sightseeing, while the other stops along
the way can be explored at a more
relaxed pace.

Day 1: Nîmes

Make an early start, because there's lots
to see in Nîmes. Begin at the Porte

d'Auguste, with its vast central arch, to enter the Old City like a Roman legionary travelling the Via Domitia, which linked the city with Rome. Then visit the Maison Carrée, the small but superbly preserved Roman temple which dates from around 5 AD. Cross over to a much more modern temple to the arts, the Carré d'Art, before walking down the Rue de l'Étoile to the vast 1st-century amphitheatre. In the afternoon, spend some time in the Musée des Beaux-Arts or, if you have the energy, climb to the top of the Tour Magne for a fine panorama of the city and of Mont Ventoux.

Day 2: Aigues-Mortes
Take a train or bus to Aigues-Mortes, walk round its 13th-century ramparts, then travel on to Montpellier. Plan to stay two nights here, as the regional capital has plenty to see and do.

Day 3: Montpellier
You can explore lively Montpellier on foot, as most of its key sights are within the mainly traffic-free streets of the Old Quarter, but to make the most of your time consider joining one of the guided tours which can be reserved through the city's tourist office. Place de la Comédie is Montpellier's hub, and pausing here for an *apéro* (aperitif) in one of its cafés is *de rigueur*. Visit the Musée Fabre for its collection of works by some of France's finest painters, including Delacroix, David and Dufy, and the Musée Languedocien, and

The ancient and scenic Aigues-Mortes

climb to the parapet of the Arc de Triomphe, built for Louis XIV, for a view of the city. Do some shopping in the 'Îsle aux Créateurs', a new and growing small quarter of studios and shops selling pottery, paintings, carving and other decorative arts, and take a quick look at the Quartier Artisanal (Artisans' District), the very oldest part of the city, where some buildings are more than 800 years old. For contrast, you might also want to visit the futuristic Antigone complex, a remarkable slice of modern architecture.

Days 4 and 5: Sète and Cap d'Agde

Arrive in Sète in plenty of time for a leisurely seafood lunch in one of the quayside restaurants along the Canal Royal, then go on to Cap d'Agde for an overnight stay followed by a day lazing on one of the region's best beaches.

Day 6: Narbonne

From Cap d'Agde, take the train to Béziers and visit the Romanesque Cathédrale Saint-Nazaire, which looms over the Old Quarter. Then carry on to Narbonne, where the must-see sight is the ornate Palais des Archevêques (Palace of the Archbishops). The Cathédrale de Saint-Juste et Saint-Pasteur is another must.

Day 7: Perpignan

For a taste of the exotic, stop at the Réserve Africaine de Sigean on your way to Perpignan. Lions, rhinos and other fearsome African beasts occupy this 300-hectare (740-acre) park, and a visit on foot takes about three hours. You can then continue your journey to Perpignan to see the Palais des Rois de Majorque.

Two weeks: Haut-Languedoc and the Canal du Midi

This itinerary combines easy walking (10–15km/6–9 miles per day) with some more challenging stretches of trail, followed by a week to relax and recover afloat. Modern canal cruise boats can be chartered at several bases along the Canal du Midi.

Day 1

Travel to the old-fashioned spa town of Lamalou-les-Bains, accessible by public transport from Montpellier, Béziers or Nîmes.

Day 2

Follow the GR7 walking trail from Lamalou-les-Bains to Héric, passing between the peaks of Mont-Caroux and Saint-Martin-l'Arcon.

Day 3

With Héric as a base, explore the spectacular Gorges d'Héric.

Day 4

Walk from Héric to Fraïsse-sur-Agoût, crossing the toughest section of the trail, the Col de Fontfroide.

Day 5

Continue on foot to La Salvetat.

Day 6

Take a rest day in La Salvetat, visit the Romanesque church with its famous 'black virgin', and then spend the afternoon lazing and swimming in the Lac de la Raviège, just outside the village.

Day 7

Bus from La Salvetat to Béziers to collect your canal cruiser.

Days 8–14

Travel from Béziers to Carcassonne by boat, with overnight stops at Capestang,

Homps (for a side-trip to Minerve), Trèbes and finally Carcassonne.

Longer

With more than a fortnight to spare, combine Haut-Languedoc and the Canal du Midi (*see above*) with a journey by car, train or bus through the upper Aude valley and the Pyrénées (*see below*). At the end of this journey, it is possible to travel home either from Perpignan or from Girona, just across the Spanish border.

Day 15

Travel from Carcassonne to Limoux to sample its famous *blanquette* sparkling wines, then stay overnight at Alet-les-Bains with its ruined abbey, medieval houses and thermal springs.

Day 16

Go on the Via Couiza to Rennes-le-Château and the peculiar church which forms the basis for an array of conspiracy theories.

Day 17

Travel east through the Corbières, visiting the Cathar castles at Quéribus and Peyrepertuse, then stay overnight in Perpignan.

Days 18–20

Relax by the sea in Collioure, on the Côte Vermeille near the Spanish border.

Stop for a spot of lunch in Limoux

Montpellier, Nîmes and northern Languedoc

Languedoc-Roussillon's northeast corner, separated from neighbouring Provence by the river Rhône, is perhaps the most exciting and contrast-filled part of the entire region. At its heart are two charismatic cities – one of them the capital of the region, the other a city with its roots deep in the Roman imperial past – while along its Mediterranean shoreline there are lively resorts and long stretches of uncrowded sands.

To the east lie the wetlands of the Camargue, where one of France's mightiest rivers, the Rhône, flows into the Mediterranean. This is a region of lagoons, water-meadows and river channels, frequented by flamingos, white horses and black bulls, and home to flamboyantly dressed horsemen and a unique local culture. Just a few miles from this area of natural heritage, the modernistic pyramids of one of Europe's first purpose-built holiday resorts overlook marinas full of yachts and motor cruisers, and a long chain of sandy beaches stretches south to a vast lagoon which is famed for producing the region's finest shellfish.

Heading north, the region embraces some of the most thinly populated and least-visited areas of Languedoc-Roussillon, with fewer historic sights and purpose-built visitor attractions but plenty of appeal for wildlife lovers, walkers and explorers looking for a holiday well off the beaten track.

Montpellier

The lively city of Montpellier, the regional capital of Languedoc-Roussillon, is one of the most attractive cities in France. A large student population, centred on a university which was founded in 1220, gives it a youthful buzz all year round. Founded in 985 AD, Montpellier is France's eighth-largest city, with a population of around 250,000, and forms the core of

Montpellier's very own Arc de Triomphe

a coastal conurbation with a population of around half a million people.

The city's natural hub is Place de la Comédie, lined with cafés and overlooked by a stylish 19th-century theatre from which it gets its name. From here, Rue de la Loge leads to another striking piece of 19th-century architecture, the Préfecture, and to the east end of Rue Foch, another upmarket shopping street. At the upper end of Rue Foch stands the Arc de Triomphe, embellished with reliefs which celebrate the military victories of the armies of Louis XIV. A statue of the Roi Soleil ('Sun King'), on horseback, stands near Place du Peyrou, a landscaped plateau of lawns, trees and ornamental flowerbeds.

East of Place de la Comédie, the Quartier Antigone district presents a dramatic contrast to the historic centre. Designed by the Catalan architect Ricardo Bofill, it draws on classical

Montpellier, Nîmes, Béziers and Narbonne area

architecture, but manages to look strikingly futuristic.

*Montpellier Office de Tourisme,
30 allée Jean de Lattre de Tassigny.
Tel: (0467) 60 60 60.
www.ot-montpellier.fr*

Agropolis-Museum

This unusual museum focuses on farming, nutrition and horticulture around the world and through the ages, with special emphasis on local agriculture and viniculture.

*951 avenue Agropolis. Tel: (0467) 04 75 00.
www.museum.agropolis.fr. Open:
Wed–Mon 2–6pm. Admission charge.*

Aquarium Mare Nostrum
(Aquarium of the Mediterranean)

This superb modern aquarium features tropical fish, penguins and other marine creatures from coral reefs, polar seas and the deep abysses of the world's oceans.

*Allée Ulysse-Odysseum.
Tel: (0467) 13 05 50.
www.aquariummarenostrum.fr.
Open: Sept–Jun Sun–Thur 10am–7pm,
Fri–Sat 10am–8pm; Jul & Aug daily
10am–10pm. Admission charge.*

Cathédrale de Saint-Pierre

This attractive place of worship, with a façade graced by twin towers topped by conical spires, was originally the church of the city's Benedictine monastery. Work began on its construction in 1364 and it was consecrated as a cathedral in 1536. It was extensively damaged during France's 16th- and 17th-century wars of religion and was rebuilt in the later 17th century.

*Rue du Cardinale de Cabrière.
Tel: (0467) 66 04 12.*

Montpellier's Place de la Comédie provides entertainment aplenty

The impressive Préfecture dominates Rue de la Loge

www.catholique-montpellier.cef.fr.
Open: Mon–Sat 9am–noon & 2.30–7pm,
Sun 9am–1pm. Free admission.

Musée Fabre (Fabre Museum)

Founded in 1825 by the Montpellier-born artist François-Xavier Fabre, the city's major art museum was extensively restored in 2007. Paintings by Vernet, David, Bassano, Veronese, Bruegel, Delacroix, Rubens and dozens of others make it the most important art collection in Languedoc-Roussillon.
39 boulevard Bonne Nouvelle.
Tel: (0467) 14 83 00.
www.ot-montpellier.fr. Open: Tue &
Thur–Sun 10am–6pm, Wed 1–9pm,
Sat 11am 6pm. Closed: Mon.
Admission charge.

Musée Languedocien
(Languedoc Museum)

Housed in an attractive 15th-century palace, this museum features prehistoric, Egyptian and classical Greek relics, and also an interesting collection of Gallo-Roman and Gothic sculpture and medieval ceramics.
7 rue Jacques Coeur, Place de la
Comédie. Tel: (0467) 52 93 03.
www.musee-languedocien.com.
Open: Mon–Sat 2.30–5.30pm.
Closed: Sun.

Parc Zoologique Henri de Lunaret
(Henri de Lunaret Zoo)

Created in 1910, Montpellier's zoo is one of the largest zoological parks in Europe, and with 80 hectares (198 acres) of paddocks and enclosures and 11km (nearly 7 miles) of walkways, it is the city's largest green space. Stars of the collection of more than 500 animals include lions, zebras, bears, and a large troop of Madagascan lemurs.
50 avenue Agropolis. Tel: (0467) 54 45 23.
www.zoo-montpellier.fr. Open: Apr–Nov
Tue–Fri 10am–6.30pm, Sat & Sun
10am–7pm. Closed: Mon.
Free admission.

Walk: Montpellier's historic centre

This walk begins with a panoramic view of the city, carries on to the city's liveliest square, and finishes in the Champs de Mars, an ideal spot for a picnic. There are plenty of opportunities for window-shopping and café-hopping.

The walk covers around 1km (²/₃ mile) and should take around an hour.

Start in the hilltop park of Place du Peyrou.

1 Place du Peyrou

In this immaculately laid-out civic garden on the western edge of the Old City, lawns, paths and flowerbeds are shaded in summer by plane and lime trees, and there are sweeping views from its southern and northern sides. From the west a domed, pagoda-like pavilion stands at the end of the massive Aqueduc Saint-Clément, a remarkable feat of 18th-century engineering, which originally carried fresh water into the city from the hills beyond. In the middle of the square is a grandiose statue of Louis XIV – a replica, placed here in 1838 on the plinth of the original bronze statue of the 'Sun King,' which was toppled, like most other royal monuments, in the early years of the Revolution.
From the east side of the gardens, cross Boulevard du Professeur Louis Valleton to get to the west end of Rue Foch.

2 Arc de Triomphe

Louis XIV's sycophantic court architects designed this monument to his victories in mimicry of the great triumphal arches of the Roman emperors. The revolutionaries who pulled down his statue left the arch, which a few years later inspired the Arc de Triomphe in Paris, erected to commemorate the triumphs of Napoleon. Rue Foch is named after Maréchal Ferdinand Foch, supreme commander of the French army during World War I.
Walk down the north side of Rue Foch for less than 50m (55yds), past the grand façade of the Palais de Justice. Turn left on to Rue du Plan du Palais, then almost immediately turn right on the narrow Rue du Palais des Guilhem. After only a few steps, enter Place de la Canourgue.

3 Hôtel de Richer

Place de la Canourgue is surrounded by ornate 17th- and 18th-century buildings. On its east side is the most impressive of all: the Hôtel de Richer, which until the Revolution was the city's town hall.

Continue east on Rue du Palais des Guilhem for 100m (110yds) to the junction of Rue Foch, Rue du Palais des Guilhem and Place des Martyrs de la Résistance. With the grand 19th-century Préfecture building on your left, continue downhill on Rue de la Loge for less than 100m (110yds) to Place Jean Jaurès.

4 Place Jean Jaurès

This café-lined quadrangle is a good place to stop for a cool drink. Midway down stands a statue of Jean Jaurès, who founded France's first socialist party and the left-wing newspaper

L'Humanité, and was murdered by a right-wing assassin in 1914.

It's a 150m (165yd) walk down to Place de la Comédie.

5 Place de la Comédie

The 19th-century Opéra building dominates the south side of Montpellier's urban hub.

Turn left (north) and walk the length of Place de la Comédie to enter the Champs de Mars.

6 Champs de Mars

The largest green space in the city centre is a pleasant, landscaped park, overlooked by a 17th-century citadel and by the Corum building, containing a vast modern opera hall.

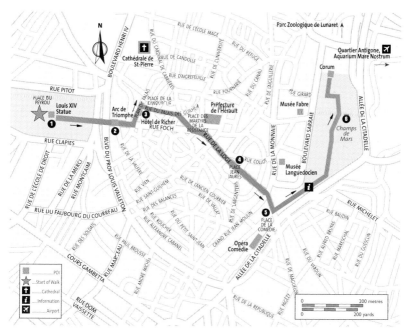

The statue of Jean Jaurès in Montpellier

Nîmes

With its treasury of Roman architectural remains, Nîmes makes some of the region's merely medieval locations look positively youthful by comparison. A vast arena, once used for gladiatorial combat, still serves as a venue for the bullfights for which Nîmes is renowned. A stone archway marks the spot where the great Via Domitia highway, linking Rome with its provinces in Gaul and Iberia, entered the city walls. In the heart of the city stands one of the best-preserved Roman temples in the world. Just outside the centre, another ancient temple is one of the highlights of a beautifully designed 18th-century park, and not far from the city a remarkable aqueduct is yet another monument to the skills of Roman engineers.

The city centre is also adorned by some more modern architectural and artistic treasures, including a gleaming art gallery designed by one of the world's leading contemporary architects. Place d'Assas, a tranquil, water-themed public sculpture space, created by Martial Raysse in 1989, features two huge stone faces, which represent the twin male and female semi-deities Nemausa and Nemausus, as well as a graceful fountain where twin child statues, also representing these water spirits, pose beneath sparkling water.

The narrow streets and squares of the older part of town have enough bars, restaurants, shops and cafés to satisfy even the most demanding visitor. The lively café-crammed Place du Marché is

HOME OF DENIM

In 1853, a young German entrepreneur, Levi Strauss, who had emigrated to California to seek his fortune, started making hard-wearing canvas trousers for gold miners. When the tough prospectors complained that the canvas pants were uncomfortable, Strauss started using an equally durable but less harsh fabric: *serge de Nîmes* soon became known in English as 'denim'. The rest, of course, is fashion history. Nîmes was a weaving centre for centuries, while Languedoc was also a centre for the growing of woad, which – until the advent of imported indigo and, later, the invention of artificial colours – provided the city's weavers with a deep blue dye. Cotton replaced silk as the favoured fibre of the city's weaving mills in the 19th century, and Nîmes' wealthy 'denim lords' endowed the city with a number of dignified mansions, built on the profits of the textile industry.

a pleasant place for breakfast, coffee, lunch, dinner or drinks.

Nîmes is an inland city, but there are beaches not far away. On summer weekends, locals flock to the seaside at La Grande-Motte and Le Grau du Roi, around 50km (31 miles) south of the city, or to the even emptier strands of the Camargue, about 60km (37 miles) to the southeast. Visitors should be aware that this migration often creates kilometres-long *bouchons* (traffic jams) on roads leading to the beaches. If planning a day out by car, get up really early and come back to Nîmes late in order to beat the crowds.

Les Arènes

With its oval of arcaded walls, 21m (68ft) high and 133m (436ft) across, the great arena is one of the most immediately impressive ancient relics in France and indeed in the world – a powerful reminder of the grandeur and power of the Roman Empire in its glory days. It was built in the late 1st century, when Rome had consolidated its hold on Gaul, and Nîmes was one of the western empire's most important cities. Tiers of stone seats could accommodate more than 20,000 people – and sometimes, for major events, still do. As Rome's power waned, the Visigoths, who settled the region in the 5th and 6th centuries, used the arena as a ready-made stronghold, and over the following centuries a densely populated community grew up within its walls and beneath its arches. Under Napoleon Bonaparte's early 19th-century empire, France was seized by a passion for restoring Roman monuments, and Les Arènes was purged of its slum-dwellers and traders

Les Arènes in Nîmes rivals any Roman amphitheatre in the world

and returned to its original role as a venue for grand public events. A self-guided tour, with optional narration in several languages using audio guides, which can be rented at the ticket office, takes the visitor from the days of the gladiators to the modern-day spectacle of the *corrida* (bullfight).

Entrance: Boulevard des Arènes (opposite Rue Fresque). Tel: (0466) 21 82 56. www.arenes-nimes.com. Open: normally Jan, Feb, Nov & Dec daily 9.30am–5pm; Mar & Oct daily 9am–6pm; Apr–Sept daily 9am–6.30pm; Jun daily 9am–7pm; Jul & Aug daily 9am–8pm. Last audio-guide rental one hour before closing. Closed: occasionally for bullfights and other major events. Admission charge.

Carré d'Art
(Contemporary Art Museum)

Designed by the acclaimed British architect Norman Foster and built in 1993, this gleaming modernist cube of glass and steel presents a stark contrast to the ancient Maison Carrée which faces it across the square. Within is an outstanding and still-growing collection of work by modern artists, from the 1960s to the 21st century. In addition to its permanent collection of some 400 paintings, prints, sculptures and installations, the museum also provides a venue for three major visiting exhibitions each year.

16 place de la Maison Carrée. Tel: (0466) 76 35 70. www.nimes.fr. Open: Tue–Sun 10am–6pm. Closed: Mon. Admission charge.

Les Jardins de la Fontaine (Fountain Gardens) and the Tour Magne (Great Tower)

A couple of minutes' walk west of the Old Town, at the north end of Avenue Jean Jaurès, the Jardins de la Fontaine are among the most beautifully designed and tranquil public spaces in France. This hemisphere of immaculate, tree-shaded gravel paths, lined with marble statues of bearded demigods and naiads, ponds and cascades where stone nymphs and cupids frolic is a marvellous example of a formal 18th-century garden. From its north side, grand double stairs sweep up to the foot of Mont Cavalier, the wooded hill which overlooks all of Nîmes. Atop the hill stands the eight-sided Tour Magne, the city's most prominent relic of Roman grandeur. From the top of the 32m

The peaceful Jardins de la Fontaine in Nîmes

(105ft) tower, there are knockout views over ancient and modern Nîmes, and on a clear day (more likely in spring or autumn than in the summer heat-haze) the massive peak of Mont Ventoux can be seen far off on the northeast horizon.

Maison Carrée (Square House)

This temple dominates what was once the forum, or main square, of Roman Nîmes. Dating from the 1st century, it was at first surrounded by a colonnaded porch, where the citizens could shelter and carry on their business in inclement weather. It was at first dedicated to Gaius and Lucius, the adopted heirs of Emperor Augustus, and is the best preserved of the temples of the long-vanished Roman-Greek Mediterranean world. That said, it has a typically Roman sturdiness, emphasised by its massive Corinthian columns, and lacks the grace of many less well-preserved classical temple ruins.
Place de la Maison Carrée.
Tel: (0466) 21 82 56. www.arenes-nimes.com. Open: Jan, Feb, Nov & Dec daily 10am–1pm & 2–4.30pm; Mar daily 10am–6pm; Apr, May & Sept daily 10am–6.30pm; Jun daily 10am–7pm; Jul & Aug daily 10am–8pm; Oct 10am–1pm & 2–6pm.
Admission charge.

Musée des Beaux-Arts (Fine Arts Museum)

Pride of place in Nîmes' Fine Arts Museum goes to an extensive mosaic,

The haughty Maison Carrée

The Marriage of Admetus, which originally formed part of a Roman villa, became buried beneath the later medieval marketplace, and was rediscovered in the 18th century. The museum also boasts a large collection of works by 18th- and 19th-century French painters as well as a number of pieces by Dutch and Flemish artists of the 17th and 18th centuries.
Rue de la Cité Foulc. Tel: (0466) 67 38 21. www.ville-nimes.fr. Open: Jan–Jun & Sept–Dec Tue–Sun 10am–6pm (until 9pm second Tue each month); Jul & Aug Tue 10am–9pm, Wed–Sun 10am–6pm. Closed: Mon. Admission charge.

Walk: Roman Nîmes

Not many places can match Nîmes for such a concentration of outstanding relics of the Roman Empire packed into such a small and eminently pedestrian-friendly area. The ongoing redevelopment of the city centre between Les Arènes and the Roman Porte d'Auguste will make this an even more attractive stroll.

Allow a couple of hours to cover the 2.2km (1½ miles) of the walk.

Start at Place du Marché, in the heart of the Old Quarter.

1 Place du Marché

In the fountain at the centre of this square lurks an alarmingly lifelike effigy of a crocodile. When Emperor Augustus Caesar founded a *colonia* (settlement) of legionary veterans here, their mascot was the crocodile, which became the city's symbol too. The modern fountain is the work of 20th-century sculptor Martial Raysse. *Walk south a short way (less than 100m/110yds) to Boulevard des Arènes.*

2 Les Arènes

Nîmes' arena is the most impressive Roman amphitheatre in the world, beating even the Coliseum in Rome. *Turn right on Boulevard des Arènes to walk anticlockwise around the amphitheatre for around 200m (220yds). On your left, on the corner of Boulevard de la Libération and Boulevard des Arènes, stands a statue of a matador.*

3 Statue of Nimeño II

This is a memorial to Christian Montcouquiol (1954–91), also known as 'Nimeño II' (his brother, later his manager, was Nimeño I). His 22-year-long bullfighting career reached its zenith in Nîmes in May 1989, when he killed six bulls in one day, and ended four months later when he was tossed and severely injured. Partially paralysed despite two years of therapy, he hanged himself in 1991. Local people still leave bouquets of flowers around his statue. *Turn left on Boulevard de la Libération and walk north, with Les Arènes on your left. After about 500m (545yds), at the junction with Boulevard de Prague, cross the street and continue north on Boulevard de L'Amiral Courbet. Cross Rue Nationale. On your left is another Roman relic.*

4 Porte d'Auguste

The Gate of Augustus is named for Rome's first emperor, Augustus Caesar. He turned Nîmes into a major provincial capital, and this ancient arched gateway is where the great highway from Rome entered the city. After the collapse of the Roman Empire, the gateway was gradually built over. It was rediscovered in the 18th century. *Turn left on Rue Nationale and walk southwest to the cathedral, and Place aux Herbes, which you cross to reach Rue de la Madeleine, along which you walk west for 150m (165 yds) to Rue Fresque. Turn right, then left on to Rue de l'Horloge, which leads you to another iconic Roman monument.*

5 Maison Carrée

The best-preserved Roman temple in the world dominates the square, originally the Roman forum (*see p35*).

From the west side of the square, turn right on Boulevard Daudet and continue along here for about 100m (110yds), then left on to Quai de la Fontaine and follow this leafy boulevard west for around 200m (220yds) to the Jardins de la Fontaine.

6 Jardins de la Fontaine

Pools, streams and faux-classical statues adorn this elegant public garden. At the northwest corner stand the elegant, dilapidated arches of the Temple of Diana.

From here, energetic walkers can hike up wooded Mont Cavalier to the Tour Magne (see pp34–5). Alternatively, retrace your steps along Quai de la Fontaine to return to the town centre.

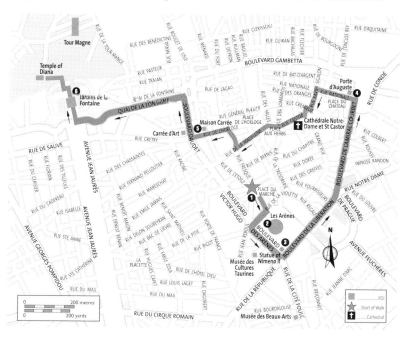

Musée des Cultures Taurines (Bullfighting Museum)

Love it or hate it, hotly debated *tauromachie* (bullfighting), also known by its Spanish name, *corrida*, is a fact of life in and around Nîmes. This modern museum (opened in 2002) may be seen as glorifying the bullfight with its exhibitions of *corrida*-related posters and paintings, glittering matadors' and picadors' costumes, swords and lances, but it also sheds light on a long tradition that stretches all the way back to Roman times, when exotic beasts were imported from all over the empire to face armed gladiators or be goaded to fight each other.

The exhibition also celebrates some of the region's less controversial forms of *la bouvine*, such as the bull-running events in which participants try to seize coloured rosettes from between the horns of young bullocks.

6 rue Alexandre Ducros.
Tel: (0466) 36 83 77. www.ville-nimes.fr.
Open: Tue–Sun 10am–6pm.
Admission charge.

Le Pont du Gard (Gard Bridge)

The Pont du Gard is an amazing example of Roman civil engineering and one of the region's best-known landmarks. Constructed in the 1st century, it was part of an aqueduct system which carried fresh water to Nîmes from the Eure river, some 50km (31 miles) from the city. Poised some 49m (160ft) above the river Gard, it is 275m (902ft) in length. Long after it ceased to serve as an aqueduct, it was used as a footbridge, and like many Roman relics it was also used as a source of ready-cut stone by local builders. Restoration work began in the 18th century and continues to the present day. An on-site museum highlights the reconstruction and the techniques used by the original Roman builders.

24km (15 miles) northeast of Nîmes.
Tel: 0820 90 33 30. www.pontdugard.fr.
Museum open: daily 9.30am–7pm.
Admission charge.

Uzès

This attractive small town is renowned as Languedoc-Roussillon's 'truffle capital', and its annual truffle market attracts buyers from all over France. The historic centre is built around a picturesque medieval castle, the seat of the De Cressol dynasty, and the Old

The once-forbidding ramparts of Aigues-Mortes

Town's squares and narrow streets are graced by the carved stone façades of 16th- and 17th-century buildings. The town's other key landmark is the Tour Fenestrelle, the 42m (138ft)-tall belfry of the Cathédrale Saint-Théodorit on Place de l'Évêché. Dating from the 12th century, this is all that remains of the original cathedral, which was destroyed during the 16th-century wars of religion (when Uzès became an extreme Protestant stronghold). The present-day cathedral was rebuilt between the 17th and 19th centuries.

25km (15½ miles) north of Nîmes. Office de Tourisme, Chapelle des Capucins, 1 place Albert. Tel: (0466) 22 68 88. www.uzes-tourisme.com

Refreshments on offer at La Grande-Motte

Le Duché

With its turrets and banners, the ducal castle (which is still home to the aristocratic De Cressol family) is straight out of a medieval romance. The oldest parts date from as early as the 11th century, and its three towers loom over a quadrangle of walls and – along with the nearby Tour Fenestrelle – dominate the skyline of the historic centre. Within, lofty salons are packed with valuable antiques and hung with tapestries, and from the top of the Donjon (the castle's highest tower) there are great views of the Old Town and its surroundings.

Place du Duché. Tel: (0466) 22 18 96. www.uzes.com. Open: Jul–mid-Sept daily 10am–1pm & 2–6.30pm; mid-Sept–end

Jun daily 10am–noon & 2–6pm. Admission charge.

Haras National d'Uzès (Uzès National Stud Farm)

Founded by Louis XIV, France's national stud farm is home to highly trained and very handsome thoroughbred mares and stallions, and a visit is a must for anyone who loves horses. There are dressage displays every Wednesday in summer (contact the Office de Tourisme for times).

Mas de Mèze, Route d'Alès. Tel: (0466) 22 68 88. Open: late Jun–mid-Sept Mon–Sat 8.30am–noon & 2–5pm (90-minute guided tours Tue & Thur); rest of the year, visits by arrangement with Uzès Office de Tourisme. Admission charge.

The *gardians* of the Camargue

With his broad-brimmed black hat, boots, velvet jacket and moleskin trews, set off by a shirt printed with vivid colours – primary red, yellow and bright blue are favourites – the Camargue *gardian* in festival costume is a uniquely picturesque character.

The tradition of *les gardians* – sometimes nicknamed 'the cowboys of the Camargue' – dates from the early 16th century. The bitter winters, scorching summers, endemic malaria and swampy marshlands made the Camargue a hard place to live until well into the 20th century, and so fostered a hardy breed of cattle herders and a unique folklore.

The *gardian's* traditional home is a tiny, one- or two-roomed thatched cottage. Its roof is thatched with reeds from the marshes, and to keep out the summer heat and winter gales it has no windows. His mount is the sturdy, semi-wild white horse which is found only in the water-meadows and prairies of the Camargue. Some of the ancestors of these steeds may have roamed southern France 20,000 years ago or more, but it's more likely that the strongest strain in their genes is from the North African Barb breed – perhaps brought here by Moorish invaders as early as the 9th century, or brought back from the Crusades by followers of Louis IX. The Camarguais horse did not receive official recognition as a breed in its own right until 1967. The ponies of the Camargue traditionally roam semi-wild in as many as 30 herds, each

A hardy *gardian* rounds up the bulls and horses

The strikingly horned local bulls are not to be messed with

dominated by a single stallion, and are rounded up by teams of *gardians* each year, when mares and newborn foals are looked over and the most promising are picked out to be trained as *gardian* steeds.

Mounted on his white horse, the *gardian's* other duty is the breeding and rearing of the black cattle of the Camargue, and the tool he uses for this work is a long-shafted trident. Like the region's white horses, the tough Camarguais cattle seem to be the descendants of some of the very first beasts to be domesticated by early humans. The strongest and most aggressive of the bulls that are reared on the Camargue ranches are destined for death in the bullrings of Nîmes, Béziers and Spain. Luckier bullocks are used in less lethal events, in which unarmed participants try to snatch coloured rosettes or ribbons from their horns.

But the colourful folklore of the *gardian* is much less ancient and deep-rooted than it appears, and owes a great deal to just one man: the Marquis de Baroncelli (1869–1943). Born in Arles of French-Italian descent, he was fascinated by the culture of the Camargue and, after moving to the region to set up his own *manade* (ranch), he also created, more or less from scratch, the costume that is now thought of as the 'traditional' *gardian* outfit. He even specified that no true *gardian* should ever be mounted on anything but a white Camarguais horse, and that on festival days he should appear in full costume, complete with a pretty girl, also dressed to the nines, sitting on the crupper of his saddle.

Jardin Médiéval (Medieval Garden)

Within the walls of the former bishop's palace, this re-creation of a herb garden of the Middle Ages is a charming spot, with shady nooks, attractive mural paintings, and neatly laid-out paths lined with beds of aromatic plants and flowers.

Impasse Port Royal. Tel: (0466) 22 38 21. www.uzes.fr. Open: Apr–Jun & Sept Mon–Fri 2–6pm, Sat & Sun 10.30am–12.30pm & 2–6pm; Jul & Aug daily 10.30am–12.30pm & 2–6pm; Oct daily 2–5pm. Admission charge.

Musée du Bonbon Haribo (Haribo Sweets Museum)

Housed in the buildings of a former mill, this museum recounts the history of one of Europe's best-known confectionery brands, with a vast assortment of sweets in every conceivable colour and flavour to taste and buy.

Pont des Charettes. Tel: (0466) 22 74 39. www.haribo.com. Open: Jul & Aug daily 10am–7pm; Sept–Jun Tue–Sun 10am–1pm & 2–6pm. Admission charge.

Aigues-Mortes

The crusader-king Louis IX (Saint Louis) decreed the building of Aigues-Mortes in 1246 to give France a purpose-built seaport near the mouth of the Rhône. The idea must have seemed sound at the time, but over the next few centuries the Rhône delta gradually silted up, access to the sea became problematic and Aigues-Mortes, with its square of walls, towers and bastions, became redundant. As a result, it is one of the most picturesque historic cities in Languedoc-Roussillon

The crystal clear waters of the Bassin de Thau

A KING'S RANSOM

Louis IX, whose statue gazes over the town's main square, the Place Saint-Louis, founded Aigues-Mortes as a springboard for his campaigns against the Muslim powers of North Africa and the Levant. He sailed from here in 1248 to launch the Seventh Crusade against Muslim Egypt, which ended badly two years later when his army was wiped out at Fariskur and Louis himself was captured. It is recorded that he was eventually ransomed for 800,000 *bezants*. The *bezant* was a gold coin weighing about 4 grams, so his ransom amounted to approximately £85 million in 21st-century terms. Louis returned to France, but set off to the wars again from Aigues-Mortes in 1270. This Eighth Crusade, against the Emir of Tunis, was another fiasco, and Louis died of dysentery. Despite these failures, he was canonised as Saint Louis by Pope Boniface VIII, 27 years after his death.

(rivalled only by Carcassonne's Cité Médiévale), because its medieval ramparts have not been demolished, quarried for their stone, or swamped over the centuries by urban growth. Inside the walls, the cobbled, car-free streets are laid out on a grid pattern and are packed with cafés, restaurants and pretty shops selling colourful Camarguais textiles, pottery, prints and paintings, as well as designer clothes and accessories. That said, and despite the summer throngs, Aigues-Mortes is not entirely given over to tourism – plenty of people still live within the ancient ramparts.

36km (22 miles) south of Nîmes.
Office de Tourisme, Place Saint-Louis.
Tel: (0466) 53 73 00.
www.ot-aiguesmortes.fr

Tours et Remparts d'Aigues-Mortes (Towers and Ramparts of Aigues-Mortes)

The walk around the medieval city's long rectangle of ramparts should not be missed. The major landmark, and the gateway to the ramparts, is the squat, round Tour de Constance, originally the major strong-point of the fortifications. From here, there are regular guided walks around the walls (book in advance). Alternatively, audio guides (in English) can be rented at the entrance or at the tourist office.

Logis du Gouverneur. Tel: (0466) 53 61 55. www.monuments-nationaux.fr. Open: Sept–Apr daily 10am–5.30pm; May–Aug daily 10am–7pm. Admission charge.

La Grande-Motte

Arriving in La Grande-Motte from Aigues-Mortes, Nîmes or even Montpellier (all of which are less then 30 minutes' drive from this seaside resort) can be a slightly surreal experience, like being transported directly from the Middle Ages to a version of the future as imagined in the 1960s. La Grande-Motte was an experiment in planned resort design which began in 1967 and was completed in the early 1970s. Vast, pyramid-style holiday-apartment complexes and hotels surround its yacht-filled marina, south of which the sandy coast stretches all the way down to Montpellier's own beach suburb, Palavas. There are no major sights or visitor attractions in the resort itself, but for a beach holiday with all the trimmings – including an impressive choice of watersports – it is an excellent choice.

24km (15 miles) southeast of Montpellier.

Around the Bassin de Thau

South of Montpellier, the inland sea of the Bassin de Thau is the largest and most impressive of the region's coastal lagoons – an expanse of almost 100sq km (38sq miles) of shallow water which is famous for producing the finest shellfish in this part of France. A long, narrow spit of dunes and sandy beaches shelters the lagoon from the open sea.

Sète

Mont Saint-Clair, the 175m (574ft) hill around which the port town of Sète grew up, is clearly visible from every corner of the Bassin de Thau. Sète itself is at first less impressive, with a stretch of industrial seaport facilities occupying the outskirts of town. Inside this determinedly commercial perimeter, however, is a picturesque inner city of tall old houses painted in pastel colours, standing along a grid of canals, the most important of which is the Canal Royal. Inevitably, Sète has been nicknamed the 'Venice of Languedoc'. Until the mid-17th century, the area was almost uninhabited, but

The charming canalside houses and cafés of Sète

the completion of the Canal du Midi created a need for a new port on the Mediterranean, and Louis XIV ordained the construction of a canal to link the inner waters of the Bassin with the sea. Sète has been a thriving fishing and mercantile port ever since, and along the Canal Royal are some of the best seafood restaurants in the region. Beyond the town centre, an unbroken (and often windswept) stretch of sand and dunes sweeps south for some 12km (7½ miles) to the resorts of Marseillan-Plage and Le Cap d'Agde.

Mèze

Hemmed in by vineyards and salt marshes, Mèze is a compact little fishing village built around a harbour where yachts and motor cruisers now outnumber fishing boats. It is still, however, a great place for seafood. The shallow waters of the Bassin de Thau just north of Mèze are one vast expanse of oyster farms, and Mèze's harbourside is surrounded by fish restaurants that in summer and at weekends attract mobs of diners from all the nearby cities. There is a small sandy beach just north of the harbour, and while the warm, shallow water is not ideal for serious swimming, it is very toddler-friendly.

Musée-Parc des Dinosaures de Mèze (Mèze Dinosaur Museum Park)

In 1996, palaeontologists working on this site unearthed a remarkable collection of fossilised dinosaur eggs dating from

Fishing boats at Mèze harbour

the Cretaceous era (65 million years ago), along with other fossils. The discovery inspired the creation of this 'dino-park', with its towering reconstructed dinosaur skeletons and interactive displays. Research continues at the site, with the exciting potential for even more new discoveries from the deep past.

5km (3 miles) northwest of Mèze, signposted off the N113 coast highway. Tel: (0467) 43 02 80.
www.musee-parc-dinosaures.com
Open: Jan Sat–Sun 2–5pm; Feb–Jun & Sept daily 2–6pm; Jul & Aug daily 10am–7pm; Oct–Dec daily 2–5pm. Admission charge.

Béziers and Narbonne

The curving stretch of coastline between the Bassin de Thau and Étang de Bages et de Sigean, where the rivers Aude, Hérault and Orb and the Canal du Midi meet the Mediterranean Sea, is the most popular summer holiday region in Languedoc-Roussillon – and with good reason. There are long stretches of fine, golden sand and calm, shallow water, serviced by a chain of bustling, purpose-built holiday resorts.

During peak holiday season, from mid-June to late August, this is one of the liveliest stretches of the Languedoc-Roussillon coast, when it attracts visitors from all over France and northern Europe for longer holidays, while city-dwellers from Béziers and Narbonne flock to the coast every weekend. Watersports of all kinds are on offer here, and there's an action-packed summer schedule of traditional festivals, and sports and cultural events. Outside the peak season, this stretch of coast is much more peaceful, and from October to April long swathes of its sands are virtually deserted.

Along with the great choice of watersports, the resorts offer all kinds of accommodation from campsites to holiday apartments. Not far inland, Béziers and Narbonne are attractive historic towns, full of character, while all along the coast there are purpose-built family attractions such as zoos and aquaparks. For a summer family holiday, there are few better places in France.

Béziers

Strategically sited just where the river Orb flows into the Canal du Midi, Béziers is a striking, ancient city, dominated by one of the greatest medieval cathedrals in Languedoc-Roussillon. The lively beach resorts of the Mediterranean coast are just a short drive away, but Béziers has an urban character all of its own, with an Old Quarter below the cathedral that seems to have changed little over the centuries. Its single biggest attraction is undoubtedly the landmark Cathédrale Saint-Nazaire, but Béziers also has several interesting museums that are well worth visiting, and its covered market, built in 1897 and given a facelift in 1986, is a great place to find local delicacies. Like Nîmes, Béziers is one of France's major bullfighting centres, and while many visitors may find the *corrida* repugnant, it certainly still plays a major part in the local culture. The city's history has also had its gory moments – it was in Béziers, in

The towering Saint-Nazaire Cathedral looks down over Béziers

1209, that the Albigensian Crusade against the Cathars began, with the massacre of the townsfolk (Cathar and Catholic alike) who had dared to resist the northern French knights; the Pope had charged them with wiping out the Cathar heresy by armed force. Unlike the original cathedral, Béziers' 11th-century Romanesque Pont Vieux, which crosses the Orb just below the cathedral, survived the crusade and still carries traffic to this day.

Office de Tourisme, 29 avenue Saint-Saëns. Tel: (0467) 76 84 00. www.beziers-tourisme.fr. Open: Jun–Sept Mon–Sat 9am–12.30pm & 1.30–6pm; Jul & Aug Mon–Sat 9am–12.30pm & 1.30–6pm, Sun 10am–1pm & 3–6pm.

Cathédrale Saint-Nazaire

Built between the 13th and 15th centuries, on the site of an earlier 12th-century cathedral which was burned to the ground when the anti-Cathar crusaders sacked the city in 1209, the cathedral is a majestic Mediterranean Gothic edifice with a huge rosette window. From the terrace outside, there's a great panoramic view of Béziers and its surroundings.

Place de la Révolution. Free admission.

Musée des Beaux-Arts (Fine Arts Museum)

Béziers' Fine Arts Museum occupies two gracious historic mansions, not far away from each other, each of which

houses a different set of exhibits. The main gallery, in the Hôtel Fabregat, is home to a worthwhile collection of paintings by artists ranging from Holbein and Delacroix to De Chirico and Soutine; there are also some fine sketches and drawings by Degas, Dufy and Rodin. The museum's annexe, within Hôtel Fayet, a townhouse dating from the 16th century, is perhaps less exciting but is also worth looking at for an introduction to the work of the Béziers-born sculptor Jean-Antoine Injalbert (1845–1933) – and indeed for a glimpse into a stylish historic building.
Hôtel Fabregat, Place de la Révolution. Tel: (0467) 28 38 78. Hôtel Fayet, 9 rue du Capus. Tel: (0467) 49 04 66. www.ville-beziers.fr (both venues). Both open: Apr–Jun, Sept & Oct Tue–Sun 9am–noon & 2–6pm; Jul & Aug Tue–Sun 10am–6pm; Nov–Mar Tue–Sun 9am–noon & 2–5pm. Admission charge.

Musée du Bitterois (Bitterois Museum) and Musée d'Histoire Naturelle (Natural History Museum)

The 'Bitterois' is the historic local name for the region surrounding Béziers, and these twin museums, located in a former army barracks, are dedicated to the history, prehistory and natural history of the region. The highlights are the Roman-era relics discovered in local farmlands or hauled up from the wrecks of ancient trading vessels discovered in the shallow waters of the nearby *étangs* (lagoons) or further offshore, and the most eye-catching exhibit is a hoard of Roman silver plates unearthed by a local farmer and known as the 'treasure of Béziers'.
Caserne Saint-Jacques, Rampe du 96ème. Tel: (0467) 36 71 01. www.ville-beziers.fr. Open: Apr–Jun, Sept & Oct Tue–Sun 9am–noon & 2–6pm; Jul & Aug Tue–Sun 10am–6pm; Nov–Mar Tue–Sun 9am–noon & 2–5pm. Admission charge.

Cap d'Agde

The unpretentious little town of Agde and its much more modern sibling Cap d'Agde make an uneasy pairing. Agde, once a thriving fishing and trading port, lost its access to the Mediterranean as the Hérault river, which meets the sea here, gradually silted up. It's now a somnolent small market town. Cap d'Agde, meanwhile,

The Gothic façade of Béziers' cathedral

has blossomed since the early 1960s into the biggest purpose-built tourist resort in France. It is at first sight the epitome of a Mediterranean tourist town, with streets lined with pink-painted villas and hotels, a yacht-filled marina, palm trees and purple bougainvillea. Cap d'Agde's beach strip begins north of town, at the southern end of a seemingly endless sandy strand that stretches all the way north to Sète (*see pp44–5*), along the seaward side of the sand dune barrier that separates the Bassin de Thau (*see p44*) from the open Mediterranean. Cap d'Agde is most famous (or notorious) as Europe's nudist capital – its Quartier Naturiste (Naturist Quarter), with its own shops, bars, restaurants and campsites, caters to tens of thousands of 'textile-free' visitors each summer (*see pp54–5*).

But there is more to Cap d'Agde than nudism. For those in search of an easy-going seaside holiday base, there are few better spots along the Languedoc-Roussillon coast, and the sights of Béziers and Narbonne, as well as a plethora of family-oriented visitor attractions, are within easy reach. *29km (18 miles) east of Béziers. Office de Tourisme, Rond-Point du Bon Accueil. Tel: (0467) 01 04 04. www.en.capdagde.com*

Aqualand

Claiming to be the very first 'aquapark' built in Europe, Aqualand is part of an empire of family-oriented waterparks (there are others not far away at Saint-

UNDERWATER ARCHAEOLOGY

UNDERWATER ARCHAEOLOGY

A number of factors make the coastline around Cap d'Agde a happy hunting ground for marine archaeologists. As long ago as the 5th century BC, there was a thriving trade between Agde and other nearby ports and Greek, Phoenician and Etruscan cities in Italy and the eastern Mediterranean. With the arrival of the Romans, trade increased. Inevitably, some ships came to grief, but the shallow waters and river silt of the Languedoc ports preserved some of their cargoes, and the seabed continues to yield exciting new finds.

Cyprien Plage and Port Leucate) which offer a great day out for parents, teens and toddlers, with water slides, pools, raft runs, beaches, bars and restaurants. *Tel: (0467) 26 85 94. www.aqualand.fr. Open: mid-Jun–first weekend in Sept 10am–6pm (until 7pm Jun–Aug). Admission charge.*

Aquarium du Cap d'Agde

This colourful collection of exotic marine life is Cap d'Agde's premier purpose-built visitor attraction, with huge tanks and pools containing sharks, turtles, jellyfish, octopi and vividly coloured corals and shellfish. *11 rue des Deux Frères. Tel: (0467) 26 14 21. www.aquarium-agde.com. Open: Jun & Sept daily 10am–7pm; Jul & Aug daily 10am–11pm; Oct–May daily 2–6pm. Admission charge.*

Musée de l'Ephèbe (Ephèbe Museum)

Boasting the largest collection of locally found ancient bronze statues and

(*Cont. on p52*)

Walk: Around Béziers

This walk takes in the highlights of the city's architectural heritage, starting with a grand belle-époque theatre commemorating France's most famous playwright, visiting a landmark which is still haunted by the tragedy of the Albigensian Crusade, and allowing glimpses of an urban history that spans almost 2,000 years, from the Gallo-Roman era through the medieval period to the 19th century and the present day.

Allow two hours to cover the 1.6km (1-mile) walk at a leisurely pace, including visits to both of the museums en route.

Start at the Théâtre Municipal Molière at the top end of Allées Paul-Riquet.

1 Théâtre Municipal Molière

The florid theatre commemorates Jean-Baptiste Poquelin (1622–73), better known as Molière and probably France's best-known and best-loved playwright. As a protégé and former schoolmate of Arnaud, Prince de Conti and Governor of Languedoc, Molière presented his second-ever comedy of manners, the *Dépit Amoureux*, in Béziers in 1656. Soon after, however, he fell out of favour with de Conti, left for Paris and never returned to Languedoc.

From the front of the theatre, turn left (west) across Place de la Victoire, cross to the north side of Rue de la République, continue west for approximately 50m (55yds), then turn right on to Rue Trencavel. At the north end of this short *street, on Place de la Madeleine, is a church with a grim history.*

2 Église de la Madeleine

When the anti-Cathar crusaders attacked and took Béziers in 1209, the surviving townspeople hoped for sanctuary within the church that originally stood here. Instead, they were burned alive, on the orders of the Abbot of Citeaux, the spiritual commander of the crusade.

From Place de la Madeleine, follow Rue Paul-Riquet southwest for about 50m (55 yds) to Place Pierre Semard.

3 Les Halles

The covered market building with its decorative wrought-iron arcades is one of the most attractive market spaces in the region and is full of stands selling produce of all sorts from early morning until midday, every day except Monday.

From the southwest corner of Place Pierre Semard, follow Rue Tourventouse to the Hôtel Fayet (9 rue du Capus).

4 Hôtel Fayet

The collection within this historic mansion (*see p48*) is part of the Musée des Beaux-Arts (Fine Arts Museum). *Leaving the Hôtel Fayet, turn immediately right, then left on Rue du Gal Crouzat, at the end of which (after less than 20m/22yds) turn right into Place de la Révolution. Hôtel Fabregat sits at the corner of the square and Rue Fabregat.*

5 Hôtel Fabregat

The main collection of the Musée des Beaux-Arts is housed within this fine historic mansion (*see p48*) and you should allow at least an hour to browse among its portfolio of oils, watercolours, etchings and drawings.

Turn left on to Rue Fabregat, then almost immediately right to walk up to the Jardin de l'Évêché (Bishop's Garden) in front of Cathédrale Saint-Nazaire.

6 Cathédrale Saint-Nazaire

The cathedral's dramatic façade is the high point of this walk, and there are superb views of the Old Town, the surrounding countryside and the coast from the terrace that encircles it (*see p47*).

Return to Place de la Révolution, then from the northeast corner follow Rue Viennet (for approximately 200m/ 220yds), then Rue du 4 Septembre (for 400m/440yds) to return to Allées Paul-Riquet and the city centre.

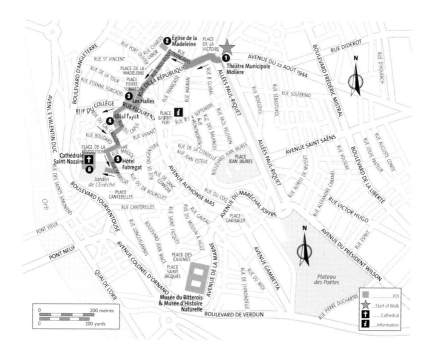

statuettes in France, this excellent small museum is Cap d'Agde's tribute to culture and heritage. It specialises in relics found on the seabed off the Languedoc coast, and in pride of place is the Ephèbe (Phoebe) of Agde, an elegant statuette of a Roman-Greek goddess discovered in the bed of the Hérault in 1964 and believed to have been made in the 4th century BC. Other exhibits include Greek and Roman amphorae and crockery, Roman statues and a number of other relics of the ancient world.

Mas de la Clape. Tel: (0467) 94 69 60. www.en.capdagde.com. Open: Jul & Aug daily 9am–12.30pm & 2.30–6.30pm; Sept–Jun Wed–Sat 9am–noon & 2–6pm, Sun 2–6pm. Admission charge.

Valras-Plage

Just south of the mouth of the river Orb, Valras-Plage is a purpose-built holiday resort that has sprung up to take advantage of one of the long swathes of sandy beach and tall sand dunes that dominate the Mediterranean coast south of the Bassin de Thau. In summer, it bustles with activity, with a 4km (2½-mile) beach, warm shallow water that is ideal for families with young children, and a great choice of watersports and other activities, ranging from sailing, kite-boarding and windsurfing to riding and fishing. Outside the peak summer season, in September and October, Valras-Plage also tempts visitors with an agenda of concerts and other cultural and sporting events including marathons and powerboat races.

13km (8 miles) southeast of Béziers on the D64. Office de Tourisme, Place René Cassin. Tel: (0467) 32 36 04. www.valras-plage.net

Domaine la Yole

This working farm allows visitors to meet farmyard animals, including horses, goats, pigs, cattle and turkeys and find out how they are raised. This being unsentimental France, visitors can also dine on locally raised meats grilled over a wood fire, accompanied by fresh vegetables and fruits from the farm's own gardens. The Domaine de la Yole also has a children's play area and a *pétanque* (bowls) court.

Route de Vendres. Tel: (0467) 30 62 93. Open: late Apr–mid-Sept Wed–Mon 9am–noon & 2–6pm. Closed: Tue. Admission charge.

Palais de la Maquette (Model Palace)

Children love this quirky, colourful collection of miniature buildings, cartoon characters, film sets and more, all of which have been painstakingly put together out of Lego and Knex model building blocks and have earned this 'Model Palace' a place in the *Guinness Book of Records*.

Résidence du Port, 11 rue du Lieutenant Panis. Tel: (0467) 39 13 53. www.palais delamaquette.com. Open: Apr–Jun & Sept daily 10am–7pm; Jul & Aug daily 10am–10pm; Oct–Dec, Feb & Mar Sat & Sun 10am–7pm. Admission charge.

Narbonne

Narbonne can claim to be the oldest of Languedoc's cities. Sited where the Aude flows into the sheltered waters of the Étang de Bages et de Sigean, it was a natural haven even before the Romans arrived. Known during the Roman era as Narbo Martius, it became the capital of their province of Galia Narbonensis, an important seaport and a major hub along the Via Domitia – the Roman

(*Cont. on p56*)

Narbonne's grand cathedral dominates the city centre

Nudist beaches and resorts

Topless swimming and sunbathing is common all over France – not just by the seaside, but on lakeside and river beaches and at open-air municipal swimming pools. Oddly enough (at least to prudish Anglo-Saxon eyes), near-nudity is more acceptable at most public and private pools than swimming in shorts, which the French regard as unhygienic.

Topless starlets sunbathing at Saint-Tropez grabbed the attention of the paparazzi in the 1960s, and there are now beaches all over Europe where nudity is acceptable – even in chilly Britain – but Cap d'Agde is the acknowledged capital of the nudist or 'textile-free' holiday lifestyle in Europe.

Cap d'Agde owes its reputation to the Germans, who were enthusiastic nudists long before the rest of Europe took to stripping off in public. In the late 1950s, a group of pioneering German nudists in search of a private spot to indulge their holiday lifestyle discovered a stretch of deserted yet perfect sandy beach next to a small vineyard. The owners allowed them to camp and, as word was passed around the textile-free world, more and more people started to arrive each summer. The vineyard's owners, the Oltra brothers, set up a formal campsite, which grew by the 1970s into a permanent resort, with hotels and apartments as well as camping and caravan sites. Nudity is allowed – indeed, encouraged – everywhere, not just on the beach but in shops, bars and restaurants, so it is the clothed (or partially clothed) who often feel out of place in the Quartier Naturiste.

These days, the 'Naturist Quarter' has informally sorted itself into straight, gay, lesbian and family sectors (it isn't difficult to tell which is which). The nucleus is the Heliopolis centre, a circle of shops, bars, restaurants and hotels immediately inland from the main beach. More hotels, shops and places to eat and drink cluster around the marina, in the Port Soleil, Port Ambonne and Port Nature complexes, and in December 2009 plans were announced to transform much of the resort into a pedestrian-only zone.

To deter *voyeurs* (and a growing clientele whom old-style naturists see as vulgar exhibitionists), many hotels and campsites insist that potential guests should be members of a recognised national or regional organisation. For first-time visitors, the official website of the Quartier Naturiste, *www.agdenaturisme.com*, lists the resort's ten commandments, starting with 'Thou shalt respect the nudity of thy neighbour' and including other rules such as 'Thou shalt not mistake naturism for exhibitionism' and 'Thou shalt not show that which you wouldn't want your relatives to be shown'.

The textile-free season begins surprisingly early. The first hardy naturists arrive in March when others are still skiing in the Pyrénées, less than two hours' drive away. More than 60,000 people visit the Quartier Naturiste each summer – but the last nude swim of the year, every 31 December, is an annual ritual that attracts a hard core of only around 200 naked bathers.

Nudism is not required everywhere in Cap d'Agde

A NEW MUSEUM FOR NARBONNE

Narbonne has quite a collection of Roman relics, ranging from graceful earthenware amphorae and stone sarcophagi to bronzes and mosaics. However, as they are divided between a number of collections in different locations – such as the Basilique de Saint-Paul and the cathedral, among others – getting to see them all can be time-consuming and the full impact of what is actually a pretty impressive collection is diluted. A new Museé de la Romanité is planned to open in 2014, gathering the most important exhibits together under one roof for the first time.

highway to Spain. It survived the collapse of the Roman Empire, but fell on hard times during the 14th century, when it was sacked by the English. Since the 17th century, the Aude has been channelled into the Canal de la Robine, which runs through the centre of town. Canal boats moor along its quays, literally in the shadow of the splendid Palais des Archevêques (*see p58*) and the adjoining Cathédrale de Saint-Just et Saint-Pasteur, reminders of the city's medieval heyday.

Basilique de Saint-Paul

This unadorned 13th-century church is not immediately impressive from the outside, but it is worth looking inside to see its incredibly ancient crypt, dating from the earliest Christian era when Narbonne was an important Roman city. Stone coffins and earthenware pots are relics of that era, as is a small Christian mosaic. All of

these may move by 2014 to a new home (*see box left*).
Rue Dupleix. www.mairie-narbonne.fr.
Open: Mon–Sat 9am–noon & 2–6pm.
Free admission.

Cathédrale de Saint-Just et Saint-Pasteur

Towering over the canal quaysides and the medieval centre of Narbonne, the city's marvellous cathedral merges with the vast Palais des Archevêques to create a complex of buildings that is unique in Languedoc and which rivals the great ecclesiastical buildings of northern France. Jackdaws roost in the cathedral's twin towers, which were constructed in 1480 – more than 200 years after work began on the cathedral. And almost eight centuries after its foundations were laid, the great cathedral remains unfinished. The original architects' grandiose plans called for part of the city's fortifications to be knocked down to create space for the building, but the Narbonnais refused to demolish the ramparts which protected them from foreign marauders, and so building came to a halt. Nevertheless, the cathedral is still tremendously impressive, both without and within, where an echoingly vast vaulted choir frames a magnificent 14th-century reredos which remained hidden for centuries until it was revealed and restored once again in 2000. It depicts hundreds of carved images of unhappy sinners enduring the torments of hell, while more

Don't miss the magnificent Palais des Archevêques while in Narbonne

deserving believers are shown being led to paradise by a benevolent Christ. Between them, those who deserve neither eternal damnation nor immediate ascent to heaven can be seen serving their time in purgatory. All in all, it's a fascinating glimpse into the mindset of medieval Christianity.

Rue Gauthier, off Place de l'Hôtel de Ville. Tel: (0468) 32 09 52. www.mairie-narbonne.fr. Open: May–Sept daily 10am–7pm; Oct–Mar daily 9am–noon & 2–6pm. Free admission.

Palais des Archevêques (Palace of the Archbishops)

The former Palace of the Archbishops is a dramatic reminder of Narbonne's past glories, albeit with a large amount of help from the great 19th-century restorer Viollet-le-Duc, who used almost as much imagination in its renovation as he did when rebuilding the medieval Cité at Carcassonne. Part of the building now serves as Narbonne's hôtel de ville (town hall), while other wings house two quite impressive museums.

On the first floor, off the central courtyard, the **Musée d'Art et d'Histoire (Art and History Museum)** has a fine collection of oil paintings, watercolours and drawings spanning four centuries of French, Italian, Spanish and Dutch art, as well as an array of fine ceramics. On the opposite side of the courtyard, in the Palais Vieux (Old Palace), the **Musée Archéologique (Archaeological Museum)** digs deeper into the region's

past, with Neolithic bone and tool fragments, Bronze Age spearheads, daggers and brooches from pre-Roman times and – most interestingly of all – some fine frescoes and mosaics from Narbonne's heyday as an important provincial capital of the Roman Empire.

Place de l'Hôtel de Ville. Tel: (0468) 90 30 54. www.mairie-narbonne.fr. Open: Apr–Sept Tue–Sun 9.30am–12.15pm & 2–6pm; Oct–Mar Tue–Sun 10am–noon & 2–5pm. Admission charge.

Narbonne-Plage

Narbonne's beach suburb is a lively spot with a long stretch of fine sand and a plentiful choice of watersports in July and August (when it gets very crowded, especially at weekends). It is located in the centre of the Parc Naturel Régional de la Narbonnaise (Narbonne Regional Natural Park), which embraces a long swathe of coastline, *étangs* (lagoons) and salt pans stretching from the mouth of the Aude river all the way south to Leucate-Plage. Inland, the Montagne de la Clape is a 17km (10½-mile) by 8km (5-mile) limestone escarpment which is almost uninhabited. Covered by *garrigue* scrub, thyme, lavender, cistus and juniper, it has its own distinctive summer aroma and is a refuge for birds, butterflies, snakes and lizards.

14km (8½ miles) east of Narbonne on the D168. Office de Tourisme, Avenue des Vacances. Tel: (0468) 49 84 86. www.narbonne-plage.com

Fontfroide Abbey is one of the region's major historic highlights

Abbaye de Fontfroide (Fontfroide Abbey)

This 11th-century abbey is one of the most impressive religious foundations in Languedoc. From its beginnings in 1093, the abbey grew in wealth and status under the Cistercian order from 1145, reaching the height of its fame in the mid-14th century. It is superbly preserved, with its abbey church, cloisters and refectory hall all in immaculate condition, and is surrounded by vineyards and an expansive rose garden which glows with red, pink, white and yellow blossoms in season. The multilingual guided tour is recommended and takes about an hour, and Fontfroide also offers wine tastings in its own restaurant.

24km (15 miles) southwest of Narbonne on the D613. Tel: (0468) 41 02 26. www.fontfroide.com. Open: Apr–Jun, Sept & Oct daily 10am–noon & 2–5pm; Jul & Aug daily 10am–6pm; Nov & Dec daily 10am–noon & 2–4pm. Admission charge.

Gruissan and Gruissan-Plage

Between Narbonne and the sea lie two shallow, brackish lagoons: the Étang de Bages et de Sigean and the smaller Étang de L'Ayrolle. They are separated by a long, narrow levee, along which flows the Canal de la Robine, which meets the Mediterranean at the southern end of the Étang de Bages et de Sigean. Salt pans occupy a wide swathe of the coastline between the lagoons and the open sea, and huge white pyramids of sea salt are typical landmarks.

Gruissan, just north of the Étang de L'Ayrolle, has more character than many of the modern, designed resorts along the Mediterranean coast. The old town – a cluster of stone houses on the inner lagoon, overlooked by a sturdy round medieval tower – is still home to a working fishing community and a fleet of small fishing boats, and presents a striking contrast to its newer beach suburb, Gruissan-Plage, which is a spread of pink-washed villas, apartment complexes and hotels, with a portfolio of five long, sandy beaches offering the usual assortment of watersports, bars and restaurants.

Réserve Africaine de Sigean (Sigean African Reserve)

The Sigean African Reserve is as close to a genuine safari experience as it is possible to find in Europe. It's much more than just a zoo, comprising 300 hectares (740 acres) of open spaces

Take in a scenic sunset at Gruissan

Watch out for rhinos at the Sigean African Reserve

where big beasts such as giraffe, rhino, elephant, lion and buffalo have space to roam. A bird lagoon is home to flocks of flamingos and pelicans, and visiting children are always charmed by the tribe of chimpanzees (who have their own private island) and by the family of frisky meerkats. The animals can be seen from your own car on an 8km (5-mile) drive through a series of savannah areas, or on foot on a walk that takes around three hours. For smaller children, there is also a hands-on petting zoo with goats, donkeys and rabbits.

6km (4 miles) north of Sigean/15km (9 miles) south of Narbonne on the D6009. Tel: (0468) 48 20 20. www.reserveafricainesigean.fr. Open: year-round 9am–dusk. Admission charge.

THE STILT-CHALETS OF GRUISSAN

Gruissan-Plage can claim to be the very first purpose-built holiday resort on the Languedoc-Roussillon coast. In the mid-19th century, well-off families from nearby Narbonne built a parade of wooden summer houses along the stretch of strand that is now known as the Plage des Chalets, and Gruissan-Plage became a fashionable summer retreat. In 1899, most of the original houses were swept away by waves raised during a devastating winter gale. In the following years, they were rebuilt, this time on wooden piles that lifted them well above the impact of the sea.

Perpignan and the Côte Vermeille

Perpignan and the surrounding region share a distinct identity that is subtly different from the rest of Languedoc-Roussillon. The region borders on the Spanish autonomous region of Catalunya (Catalonia) and there is a strong Catalan flavour to local culture, including a fondness for the traditional dance known as the sardana, and distinctive Catalan influences on the regional cuisine.

The red and yellow Catalan colours fly in many places, and road and street signs are often in both French and Catalan: Perpignan, for example, is also referred to as Perpinyà, its Catalan name. This is a region with something for everyone, with sandy beaches and purpose-built resorts as good as any on

The striking red brick of Le Castillet

THE CENTRE OF THE UNIVERSE?

Those arriving at Perpignan's railway station may be puzzled by the metre-high slogan painted on its main platform which declares: 'Perpignan: Centre du Monde' ('Perpigan: Centre of the World'). Perpignan owes this distinction to the Catalan surrealist Salvador Dalí, who claimed that the station was the centre of the universe and said that he received inspiration for much of his work while in the station waiting room. Those looking for more Dalí-esque experiences can head just across the Spanish border (by train or bus) to the moustachioed-one's birthplace, Figueres, and the amazing Teatre-Museu Dalí (Dalí Theatre Museum, *www.salvador-dali.org*), surely one of the most inspiringly weird artistic institutions in the world.

the Languedoc-Roussillon coast, but with a shoreline that offers at its southern end more rugged cliffs, crags and coves than are found along the rest of the Mediterranean coast, and a handful of former fishing villages where the Mediterranean light and colour inspired a generation of painters.

As Languedoc-Roussillon's second-largest city, Perpignan is also a major gateway to the region by air or rail, and a holiday starting here can combine the attractions of the coast with those of the Pyrénées-Orientales, which loom spectacularly on the southern skyline. Visit at the right time of year (in early summer), and you can swim and sunbathe within sight of snowcapped peaks.

PERPIGNAN AREA
Perpignan

Perpignan's history is turbulent – even by the standards of Languedoc-Roussillon's eventful past. Only 32km (20 miles) north of the Spanish frontier, and controlling the most important land route between France and the Iberian Peninsula, it inevitably played a key role through centuries of power struggles, during which it changed hands more than a few times.

Perpignan's pedigree is not as old as that of Narbonne or Béziers. Founded in the 10th century, it was the capital of the Counts of Roussillon until it fell into the hands of the Counts of Barcelona in 1172. In 1276, it became the mainland capital of the new Kingdom of Majorca, which included the Balearic Islands and lands on both sides of the Pyrénées. It was absorbed by the Spanish Kingdom of Aragon in 1344, seized by Louis XI of France in 1463, given back to Spain in 1493, conquered once again by the French in 1642 and finally handed over permanently to France through the Treaty of the Pyrénées in 1659. As a bastion of French power, Perpignan was fortified during the 17th century by Vauban, the doyen of French military engineers, but its ring of ramparts was demolished at the beginning of the 20th century to allow the city to expand, and surprisingly little survives from its militant past.

With a population of around 300,000, Perpignan is the second-

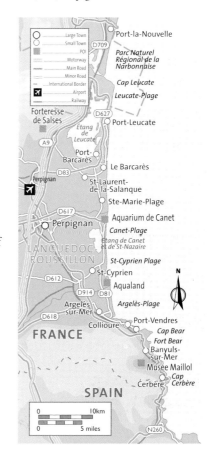

biggest urban area in Languedoc-Roussillon after Montpellier, but its historic centre is compact and easy to explore on foot, while the nearest Mediterranean beaches are only minutes away from the city centre. *Office de Tourisme, Palais des Congrès, Place Arnaud Lanoux.* *Tel: (0468) 66 30 30.* *www.perpignantourisme.com*

Le Castillet and Musée Catalan des Arts et Traditions Populaires Casa Pairal (Casa Pairal Museum of Popular Catalan Arts and Traditions)

The red-and-yellow Catalan banner flies proudly over this miniature red-brick castle, which is the only surviving remnant of Perpignan's original city walls. The first tower, guarding one of the principal gateways to the city, was built in 1368, when Perpignan was part of the Kingdom of Aragon. It was rebuilt and made even more formidable by the French between 1475 and 1485. In the 17th and 18th centuries, it was the city's main prison. It now houses the Casa Pairal Museum of Popular Catalan Arts and Traditions, featuring a collection of costumes, farming tools, household goods and antique weaponry. *Place de Verdun. Tel: (0468) 35 42 05.* *www.mairie-perpignan.fr. Open: Oct–Apr Wed–Sun 11am–5.30pm; May–Sept Wed–Sun 10am–6.30pm. Admission charge.*

Cathédrale Saint-Jean-Baptiste

The distinctive 14th-century cathedral dedicated to Saint John the Baptist is a prominent relic of Perpignan's medieval golden age. Adjoining it is the even older Saint-Jean-le-Vieux, an impressive Romanesque pile whose ancient

View over the colourful city of Perpignan

stonework is being carefully and painstakingly restored.
Place Gambetta. Tel: (0468) 51 33 72. www.perpignantourisme.com. Open: Mon & Wed–Sat 10am–noon & 2–5pm; Tue & Sun 2–5pm. Free admission.

Forteresse de Salses (Salses Fortress)

With its square of red-brick battlements, bastions and round-topped turrets, Salses is one of the most impressive fortifications in southern France – and considering that it was built in the 15th century and was besieged on numerous occasions during the Franco-Spanish wars of the 16th and 17th centuries, it is in remarkably good shape. It was built by the Aragonese as a defence against French invasion, and it served its builders well until it finally fell to France in 1642. With the Treaty of the Pyrénées, which brought peace between France and Spain, it became redundant. Like many of the fortresses of that era, it was later used as a prison. Guided tours help to bring its past to life, but it can also be visited independently.
Salses-le-Château, 15km (9 miles) north of Perpignan, off the N9. Tel: (0468) 38 60 13. www.salses.monuments-nationaux.fr. Admission charge.

Musée de l'Aviation (Aviation Museum)

Founded by former French Air Force fighter pilot Charles Noetinger (1934–95) and now run by his family, this unusual museum's collection includes an assortment of vintage military aircraft ranging from a Republic RF84 Thunderflash jet fighter to a rare British De Havilland Vampire and the 'Flying Flea', one of the smallest aircraft ever built.
Mas Palegry. Tel: (0468) 54 08 79. www.musee-aviation.com. Admission charge.

Musée Bella (Bella Museum)

She may be less well known outside France, but from 1946 to 1984 the Bella doll was the French answer to the American Barbie. This charming museum is dedicated to the dolls, created in Perpignan, which delighted generations of French children.
Espace Primavera 6, Avenue du Languedoc. Tel: (0468) 22 97 11. www.poupees-bella.com

Musée Hyacinthe Rigaud (Hyacinthe Rigaud Museum)

Founded in 1820, this fine arts museum is named after the Perpignan-born 17th century portrait painter Hyacinthe Rigaud, who worked in this historic mansion and became a favoured portraitist at the court of Louis XIV. Later, it was used as a studio by some of the most revolutionary artists of the 20th century – Raoul Dufy, Jean Cocteau and Pablo Picasso – who lived and worked here. Some of their works form the core of a modern art collection which also includes drawings and paintings by an array of their contemporaries.

(*Cont. on p68*)

Walk: Perpignan's historic centre

Perpignan's historic centre is eminently walkable, with all the major sights conveniently grouped close together. This walk allows a glimpse of its most striking historic landmarks. It culminates at the stunning Palace of the Kings of Majorca, hidden behind its formidable Vaubanesque ramparts.

Allow three hours, including visits, to cover the 1.3km (³/₄-mile) route.

Start in the city's liveliest square, Place Arago.

1 Place Arago
Place Arago, on the east side of the Basse river, which passes through town in an artificial channel, is the city's social hub. It is packed with café-bars and restaurants.
From the north side of Place Arago, follow Quai Sadi-Carnot along the east bank of La Basse for 300m (330yds) to Place de Verdun.

2 Le Castillet
This red-brick mini-fortress (*see p64*) is the only part of Perpignan's old fortifications to have escaped demolition. Catalan rebels were imprisoned here after their defeat against the French in 1674, and it now houses a museum of local culture.
From the southeast corner of the square, follow Rue du Castillet for 200m (220yds), then turn right on to Place Gambetta.

3 Cathédrale Saint-Jean-Baptiste
Construction of the cathedral began in 1324, though it did not become a cathedral until 1602. Its style employs courses of boulders alternating with layers of narrow red-brick decoration.
From the southeast corner of Place Gambetta, enter Campo Santo.

4 Campo Santo (Graveyard)
Long arcaded galleries surround this open space, consecrated as Perpignan's main cemetery during the early 14th century. The space within is now a venue for summer cultural events.
Walk south on Rue Amiral Ribeil, then turn right on Rue de la Révolution Française. Continue to the northeast corner of Place de la République, walk diagonally across the square, follow a narrow pedestrian street west, cross Rue de la Cloche d'Or and enter Rue d'Ange. On your left, you will see the Musée Hyacinthe Rigaud.

5 Musée Hyacinthe Rigaud

This museum's collection of modern art makes a welcome change from the omnipresent medievalism of the rest of the Old Town.

Return to Rue de la Cloche d'Or, turn right and walk to the south end of the street, cross Rue des Augustins and follow Rue Petite de la Monnaie for around 250m (275yds). Turn right on Rue des Remparts la Réal and at its end cross Rue des Rois de Majorque, enter Rue des Archers and follow it a short *way to the entrance of the Palais des Rois de Majorque.*

6 Palais des Rois de Majorque

The Palace of the Kings of Majorca is evocative of many centuries of troubled times when the city changed hands repeatedly between French, Spanish and Aragonese rulers.

To return to the centre of town, walk back down Rue des Archers, cross Rue des Rois de Majorque and follow Rue Grande de la Monnaie to Place du Pont d'Envestit.

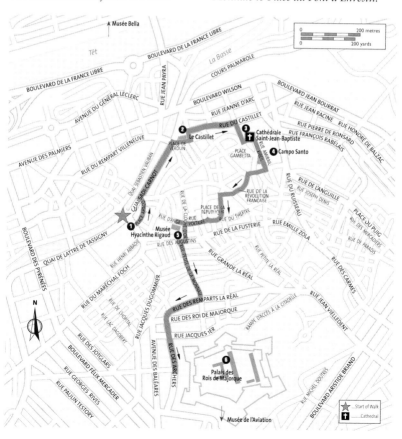

FRANCE'S MASTER MILITARY ENGINEER

Perpignan owes the ramparts that surround the Palace of the Kings of Majorca to Sébastien Le Prestre (1633–1707), later the Marquis de Vauban, who was Marshal of France and master builder of fortresses to Louis XIV, the 'Sun King'. Generally referred to simply as 'Vauban', the highly successful and acclaimed marshal created the characteristically star-shaped fortresses that revolutionised defensive warfare and proved to be virtually impregnable, securing France's frontiers from the Alps and the Rhône river to the Pyrénées. Vauban improved or built the fortifications of hundreds of cities and fortified many harbours, and the evidence of his handiwork is still clearly visible all over France today.

16 rue de l'Ange. Tel: (0468) 35 81 23. www.mairie-perpignan.fr. Open: Wed–Mon 10am–12.30pm & 1.30pm–6.30pm. Admission charge.

Palais des Rois de Majorque (Palace of the Kings of Majorca)

This 13th-century edifice is Perpignan's most impressive historic building and is the hub of the Old Quarter. It has an august pedigree, having originally been built as the mainland seat of King Jaume II of Majorca. Jaume inherited the title, along with his lands in Majorca and on the Roussillon mainland, from his father, Jaume I, Count of Barcelona and King of Aragon. The palace's grim and functional outer ramparts date from a much later military period, having been designed by Vauban (see box), chief military engineer to King Louis XIV,

following France's final conquest of the Roussillon region. Within the 17th-century fortifications, the original palace presents a more attractive face, with vaulted Gothic halls, royal apartments and chapels which are now used for occasional art exhibitions. 2 rue des Archers. Tel: (0468) 34 48 29. www.perpignantourisme.com. Open: Jun–Sept daily 10am–6pm; Oct–May daily 9am–5pm. Admission charge.

Port-Leucate, Leucate-Plage and Port-Barcarès

Between Salses and the Mediterranean lies the southernmost of the coast's chain of shallow, sheltered lagoons: the Étang de Leucate, also known as the Étang de Salses. Straddling the sand bar between the lagoon and the Mediterranean, a chain of purpose-built summer resorts stretches southward from Cap Leucate and Leucate-Plage to Port-Barcarès, where the lagoon flows into the sea. These holiday villages are aimed squarely at the mid-range family market, with apartments, campsites and mobile-home parks, watersports and aquaparks.

Aqualand

Pools for toddlers, older children, teenagers and adults and a dazzling selection of water rides and flumes are on offer here, plus a choice of places to eat and drink. Avenue du Roussillon, Port-Leucate. Tel: (0468) 40 99 98. www.aqualand.fr.

The shallow lagoon of Leucate bay

Open: third weekend in Jun–mid-Jul daily 10am–6pm; mid-Jul–end Aug daily 10am–7pm. Admission charge.

Canet-Plage

The Têt river, which flows into the Mediterranean about 13km (8 miles) east of Perpignan, was integral to that city's growth in medieval times, supplying it with a link to the sea. Perpignan's designed beach suburb, Canet-Plage, straddles the river's mouth, which provides an anchorage for yachts and motor cruisers, and the resort stretches southward from the river along a long, sandy spit of sand and dunes that cuts off the lagoon of the Étang de Canet et de Saint-Nazaire from the open sea. The lagoon attracts a range of bird species, including small flocks of flamingos, while Canet-Plage's beach has plenty of watersports during the summer season, along with a good range of bars, restaurants, shops and places to stay. Canet-Plage's tourist office proudly boasts that the resort enjoys 325 days of sunshine per year, and as a result the village stays open almost year-round.

13km (8 miles) east of Perpignan on the D617. Office de Tourisme, Espace Méditerranée. Tel: (0468) 86 72 00. www.ot-canet.fr

Aquarium de Canet

Canet-Plage's top visitor attraction is its aquarium, with dozens of tanks full of colourful and exotic freshwater and marine creatures from all the world's oceans and continents, including sharks, sea turtles, giant toads, and the coelacanth, a unique survival story from before the era of the dinosaurs.

Canet-Plage is a popular spot for flamingos

Boulevard de la Jetée. Tel: (0468) 80 49 64. www.ot-canet.fr. Open: Jan–Jun & Sept–Dec daily 10am–noon & 2–6pm; Jul & Aug daily 10am–6pm. Admission charge.

Saint-Cyprien-Plage

Like most of the resorts along this part of the Roussillon coast, Saint-Cyprien consists of an older village a little way inland and a much more modern holiday resort suburb spreading along the sandy beach. The resort of Saint-Cyprien-Plage lies between the Étang de Canet et de Saint-Nazaire and the mouth of the Tech river, which flows down from the Pyrénées to meet the Mediterranean here. Saint-Cyprien has seamlessly transformed itself from a struggling fishing and farming community into a thriving holiday spot, with a pleasure port full of yachts and

motor cruisers and 6km (4 miles) of excellent sandy beach stretching north and south of Saint-Cyprien-Plage.
8km (5 miles) south of Canet-Plage. Office de Tourisme, Quai Arthur Rimbaud. Tel: (0468) 21 01 33. www.saint-cyprien.com

Aqualand

Like its sister park at Port Leucate, this Aqualand offers an exciting choice of rides, slides and pools for all the family.
Mas des Capellans, Saint-Cyprien. Tel: (0468) 21 49 49. www.aqualand.fr. Open: third weekend in Jun–mid-Jul daily 10am–6pm; mid-Jul–end Aug daily 10am–7pm. Admission charge.

CÔTE VERMEILLE

South of the Tech river, the coastline changes dramatically as the long sandy strands that are characteristic of most of the Languedoc Roussillon coast give way to a more rugged seascape of small coves and steep cliffs of reddish rock. It is the rock that gives this stretch of coast its name: the 'Vermilion Coast'. South of Argelès-sur-Mer, the shoreline bulges eastward into the Mediterranean, and a serpentine coast road, the D914, zigzags giddily southeast, passing a series of steep headlands to Cap Cerbère and the Spanish border.

Argelès-sur-Mer

Argelès-sur-Mer and its beach annexe, Argelès-Plage, are next to the southernmost stretch of long, sandy beach on the Languedoc-Roussillon coast. This is by far the busiest holiday spot in the area, attracting hundreds of thousands of visitors every summer and providing them with all the trimmings of a mid-market family resort. The resort's main beach reaches northward towards the mouth of the Tech river while, to the south of the marina at Port Argelès, the rockier coastline of the Côte Vermeille truly begins at Racou-Plage.

Collioure

After the ever-so-slightly monotonous modern architecture and flat terrain of the beach resorts to the north, Collioure is a very welcome change. Here, rocky headlands create a postcard setting for a properly picturesque former fishing village which has lured artists since the early 20th century, when André Derain, Henri Matisse and other disciples of Les Fauves were attracted by its Mediterranean light and colour and, no doubt, by its congenial lifestyle. Visitors will find a picket line

Collioure's harbour has long been an inspiration for artists

of hack artists churning out less inspired works along the seaside esplanade during the tourist season. Rising above the harbour, the pretty old Mouré quarter with its ice-cream-coloured houses is no longer home to fisherfolk but to chic boutiques, cafés and art galleries.

This close to a frontier that was contested for centuries, Collioure's past was far from peaceful, as evidenced by two sturdy fortresses: built in the 17th century, Fort Miradou looms over the bay from the northern headland, and the 16th-century Fort Saint-Elme overlooks the village from the south. Collioure's third stronghold, the Château-Royal, is the village's most impressive landmark.

32km (20 miles) south of Perpignan. Office de Tourisme, Place 18 Juin. Tel: (0468) 82 15 47. www.collioure.com

THE 'WILD BEASTS'

The artists who nicknamed themselves Les Fauves ('Wild Beasts') rocked the established art world during their brief heyday in the first decade of the 20th century. Following on from post-Impressionists like Vincent Van Gogh and Paul Gauguin, they threw away the rule book and their work emphasised brilliant colour and exuberant brushwork over the naturalistic tones and mannered forms of conventional painters. Collioure, with its bright sunshine, blue sea and red cliffs, inspired their leading lights, Henri Matisse and André Derain, along with a generation of Fauvist followers, including such significant artists as Raoul Dufy and Georges Braque, who would later work closely with Pablo Picasso to develop Cubism.

Château-Royal

The 'royal castle' is a dramatic 14th-century pile, built originally by the Aragonese and later used as a royal residence by the rulers of the Kingdom of Majorca. It rises in three tiers above the harbour, and its outer ramparts are easily recognisable as the work of Vauban, Louis XIV's great military engineer, who strengthened the castle's defences in the late 17th century.

Tel: (0468) 82 06 43. www.collioure.com. Open: Jun–Sept daily 10am–5.15pm; Oct–May daily 9am–4.15pm. Admission charge.

Le Chemin du Fauvisme (Fauvist Path)

The Fauvist Path is a free, signposted walk that allows the visitor to follow literally in the footsteps of Derain and Matisse, with 20 reproductions of their works displayed around the village at the points where the artists painted them so that you see exactly what they saw while at work.

Starting point: Espace Fauve, Avenue Camille Pelletan. Tel: (0468) 98 07 16. www.collioure.com

Église de Notre-Dame-des-Anges

Overlooking the harbour, this church's medieval bell tower doubled for centuries as a beacon to guide vessels safely into port. It was extended in 1684, and the belfry's distinctive dome is an even later embellishment which was added in

Port-Vendres occupies a picturesque spot on the Côte Vermeille

1818. From the outside, it is a rather dour-looking building, but its interior, with its gilt-covered and elaborately carved altarpiece, is sumptuous.
Tel: (0468) 82 15 47. www.collioure.com. Open: daily 9am–noon & 2–6pm. Free admission.

Fort Saint-Elme

Built in 1552 during the reign of the Spanish king (and Holy Roman Emperor) Charles V, this hilltop stronghold was part of Spain's defences against French invasion. It is privately owned, but open to the public during the summer months.
Tel: 0664 61 82 42. www.collioure.com. Open: Apr–Sept (guided tours only) 2.30–7pm. Admission charge.

Musée d'Art Moderne (Modern Art Museum)

This dazzling modern art collection includes works by some of the leading Fauvists and a supporting cast of modern artists from the early 20th century to the present day. The museum continues to sponsor exciting new talent, and its collection is added to every year thanks to the Prix Collioure programme, which every two years awards two young artists a scholarship to live and work in Collioure on condition that they each donate one of their works to the museum.
Villa Pams, Avenue de Port-Vendres. Tel: (0468) 82 10 19. www.collioure.com. Open: Sept–Jun Wed–Mon 10am–noon & 2–6pm; Jul & Aug daily 10am–noon & 2–7pm. Admission charge.

Port-Vendres

Collioure looks like the epitome of a postcard-pretty Mediterranean fishing port, but the truth is that the picturesque, immaculately painted fishing boats that line its harbour with their sails neatly furled are no longer working vessels but carefully preserved pleasure boats. In contrast, Port-Vendres, another natural harbour between rocky headlands just south of Collioure, is still a working port, and the tuna and sardine boats that line its quaysides are solid modern workhorses that show the dents and rust of hard daily use. That said, there are few places along the coast that serve up fresher fish, and the harbourside restaurants attract discriminating seafood lovers from miles around. A visit to the fish auction is an educational experience for anyone who has only seen the fruits of the Mediterranean neatly packaged for supermarket consumption, with wriggling and writhing boxes of prawns, squid, sardines, monkfish and other even less recognisable denizens of the deep being sold off to fishmongers and restaurant buyers. Auctions are held every weekday evening (times vary depending on tides, wind and the season).

11km (7 miles) south of Collioure.

The harbour of Port-Vendres is a great place for fresh seafood

Panoramic view over Banyuls-sur-Mer and its protected Marine Reserve

Banyuls-sur-Mer and Cerbère

The pebbly beach at Banyuls is unprepossessing compared with the vast sandy strands further north, but the water is blue and clear and the place has plenty of character to make up for its lack of sand and palm trees. The seas offshore are protected as part of the Réserve Marine Naturelle de Cerbère-Banyuls (Cerbère-Banyuls Natural Marine Reserve) and offer the best scuba diving in Languedoc-Roussillon. The hinterland of Banyuls is noted for vineyards that produce a highly regarded sweet wine. Banyuls can be drunk with dessert or as an *apéro*, and several vineyards nearby offer guided tours and tastings.

Beyond Banyuls, the small fishing port of Cerbère is even less of a tourist draw, despite a picturesque setting overlooked by the jutting headland of Cap Cerbère, where a lighthouse marks the end of French territory and the border with Spain.

20km (12½ miles) south of Collioure.
Office de Tourisme, 6 place de la République, Banyuls-sur-Mer.
Tel: (0468) 88 31 58.
www.banyuls-sur-mer.com

Musée Maillol (Maillol Museum)

Banyuls-born sculptor Aristide Maillol was known for his luscious female nudes. This collection (established by his model and muse Dina Vierny) in the farmhouse which he used as his studio (and where he is buried) displays many of his most curvaceous works.

Vallée de la Roume, near Banyuls-sur-Mer. Tel: (0468) 88 57 11.
www.musee-maillol.com.
Open: Wed–Mon 10am–noon & 4–7pm.
Admission charge.

Bullfighting in Languedoc

Repulsive and needlessly cruel as it seems to many visitors, the bullfight or *corrida* (also known in French as *tauromachie*) is still seen by many local people as an essential part of the culture of Languedoc-Roussillon. Béziers, Nîmes – where bullfights are held, appropriately enough, in the ancient arena where the Romans held their own gladiatorial combats – and Céret in the Pyrénées-Orientales, are among the region's *corrida* capitals. They host high-profile *ferias* (bullfighting festivals) which attract thousands of fans and star *toreadores* from all over the bullfighting world.

Despite such popularity, the days of the *corrida* may be numbered. Though bullfighting has spread from the Iberian Peninsula to many parts of the world – including Mexico, Peru and other South American countries – it may gradually be losing ground in its original homelands. There is hot debate between those Languedociens who perceive the *corrida* as a primitive, savage ritual that should be banned, and those who fiercely defend it. In theory, bullfighting could be banned under France's laws against cruelty to animals. However, in a typically pragmatic French compromise, it is permitted because it is regarded as an 'unbroken local tradition' that stretches back for centuries – perhaps to the time of the Romans.

The debate was fuelled when in 2010 the Spanish autonomous region of Catalunya, just across the border, became the first region in mainland Spain to ban bullfighting. The decision may strengthen the anti-*corrida* lobby in Languedoc-Roussillon by weakening claims that *tauromachie* is a vital part of Catalan culture. On the other hand, it is likely to lead to many Spanish *aficionados* travelling across the border to enjoy their passion in Perpignan or Nîmes – so that the pro-bullfight faction can claim that their 'art' contributes to the local economy.

The main bullfighting seasons are February and autumn, with Nîmes hosting its annual Feria des Vendanges to celebrate the grape harvest during the third week in September.

Some visitors may find the Camargue version of the bullfight, known as the *bouvine*, less repellent and more exciting. The bull is not killed or harmed in these 'rosette races', which are held in several villages in the Petite Camargue area.

The memorial statue of bullfighting legend 'Nimeño II' (*see page 36*) in Nîmes

Instead, white-costumed contestants called *razeteurs* try to snatch a rosette from between the bull's horns. This means getting right up close to an angry animal, and the bull sometimes pursues the *razeteur* around the ring or drives him up against the perimeter wall for what is known as the *coup de la barrière*. Nîmes, too, has a similar non-lethal version of the *corrida*, called the *courses*, when a crest known here as the *cocard* must be grabbed from the beast's horns. Nîmes also hosts events known as *courses libres*, when a herd of bullocks is released into the streets and amateur participants dash ahead of them or try to snatch the *cocards* from their heads. Only the boldest visitor is likely to want to take part in one of these: arguably it takes a lot more courage to match one's unarmed reflexes with an angry bull than to face an animal that has already been weakened by the *picadores'* darts – and have the added advantage of being equipped with a sword…

Pyrénées-Orientales and Corbières

For those who love dramatic landscapes, awesome scenery and romantic ruins, this swathe of rugged territory bounded in the south by the grand peaks of the Pyrénées is perfect. Between the Aude river and the Mediterranean, the arid limestone hills of the Corbières and the Fenouillèdes were the heartland of the Cathar resistance, and the battlements of deserted castles crown many hilltops.

To the south, the foothills of the eastern Pyrénées are thickly wooded and thinly populated, rising to the high peaks of the Canigou massif and the Spanish frontier. This is above all a region of contrasts: there are pretty small spa towns nestling in the valleys of fast-flowing rivers that have their sources in the high Pyrénées, two outstanding natural parks offering mountain hiking to test even the fittest walker, romantic ruins and impressively functional border fortresses, and a human heritage that stretches from prehistoric cave-painters to the revolutionary Fauvist and Cubist painters of the early 20th century. Travelling through the landscapes of the Tech and Têt valleys, it's easy to see why the light and colour of these landscapes attracted artists like Picasso. Meanwhile, on the western fringes of the region, the enigmatic symbols of Rennes-le-Château have become an idiosyncratic magnet for thousands of New Age mystics and conspiracy theorists.

Céret

Céret nestles in the lower valley of the Tech river and takes its name from the cherry orchards which flourish in the valley's mellow microclimate. Céret claims to be France's 'cherry capital' and celebrates this with an annual Fête de la Cerise (Cherry Festival) at the end of May, when the village comes alive with hundreds of folk musicians, traditional Catalan sardana dancing, and every imaginable cherry-based product from conserves and desserts to liqueurs, cherry-flavoured beer and a menu of cherry-influenced recipes that seems to become more inventive every year. The other big event in Céret's calendar is the annual *feria* (usually

SPITTING THE PIPS

One of the high points of the cherry festival, and guaranteed to please younger visitors (and probably their parents too) is the cherry-pip spitting contest. Anyone can enter, and the current record to beat stands at 11.5m (93ft). Go for it!

held on the second or third weekend in July) when a herd of young Camargue black bullocks is run through the streets. Unlike other 'bull-running' events, in which the participants try to outrun the bulls, the runners in the streets of Céret run behind the bullocks, try to grab hold of their tails, and then hang on as long as possible.

The village's iconic landmark is the Pont du Diable (Devil's Bridge). This remarkable feat of medieval engineering, which was completed in 1341, leaps the Tech in a single 45.5m (149ft) bound. Amazed by this achievement, villagers decided that the architect could only have built the bridge by trading his soul for the aid of the Devil – hence its name.

7km (4½ miles) west of A9 junction 43 on the D115. Office de Tourisme, 1 avenue Georges Clemenceau. Tel: (0468) 87 00 53. www.ot-ceret.fr

Musée d'Art Moderne
This astonishing collection of modern art includes works by some of the Modernist giants of 20th-century arts, including Juan Gris, Marc Chagall, Henri Matisse, Joan Miró, Chaim Soutine and many more. The star of the show is of course Pablo Picasso, and the collection of his bowls and vases decorated with bulls, minotaurs and dancers clearly point to the fact that he drew some of his inspiration from Céret's long tradition of *tauromachie* ('bull-running').

(*Cont. on p82*)

Pyrénées-Orientales and Corbières

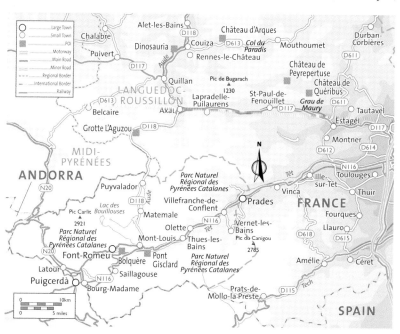

Artists in Céret

The little village of Céret seems to have become a world capital of modern art almost overnight, around a century ago, when it was discovered by a handful of artistic pioneers who found it to be cheaper, friendlier and warmer in every sense than Paris. They were drawn, of course, not just by Céret's congenial lifestyle and affordable places in which to live and work, but also by its warm and sunny microclimate. With more than 300 days of sunshine every year, blue skies and vivid colours, Céret must have been an inspiring place in which to paint.

Among the first artist-settlers was the Catalan sculptor Manolo Hugué, who arrived in 1910 and soon invited

Portrait of Picasso by Juan Gris (1912)

many of his fellow artists to join him. But Céret owes its high-profile reputation as a haven for artists primarily to the peripatetic and unbelievably prolific Pablo Picasso, who first came here in 1911, to be followed by his close friend and colleague Georges Braque, and subsequently by a cavalcade of other painters and sculptors who were involved in the Cubist movement – as well as a series of the many lovers who modelled for him, including Fernande Olivier and Eva Gouel.

Over the next decades, Céret attracted many of the 20th-century's most adventurous and influential artists, including Henri Matisse, Amadeo Modigliani, the Banyuls-born sculptor Aristide Maillol, Chaim Soutine, Juan Gris, Marc Chagall, Joan Miró and many more. During World War II, a number of artists (including Chagall, Tristan Tzara and Jean Dubuffet) came to Céret from German-occupied Paris, and many of them stayed on after the end of the war.

The founder of Céret's Musée d'Art Moderne (Modern Art Museum), Pierre Brune (1887–1956), was among the first artists to settle in the village; he moved there in 1916 to

Devil's Bridge and the Tech river in Céret

recover from the effects of an illness contracted while serving in the trenches during World War I. Brune was also one of the leaders of the group of artists who worked together in Paris in an area of studios that came to be known as the Cité Falguière. Among his colleagues was the struggling Abstract Expressionist painter Chaim Soutine (1893–1943), whom Brune invited to Céret in 1919. Soutine's stay in Céret seems to have been inspirational: in less than a year, between 1919 and 1920, he created more than 200 paintings. Soutine returned to Céret frequently in the early 1920s.

Brune's own work spans portraiture, still-life and landscapes. He returned to Céret after World War II, and, with another of Céret's artistic leading lights, the Franco-American Frank Burty Haviland (1886–1971), began in 1950 to create a remarkable portfolio of works donated by his contemporaries or their heirs. Works by Matisse and Picasso form the core of the Modern Art Museum's collections, and it is these that most visitors come to see.

The dramatic Pic du Canigou

8 boulevard Maréchal Joffre. Tel: (0468) 87 27 76. www.musee-ceret.com. Open: Jul–mid-Sept daily 10am–7pm; mid-Sept–Oct, May & Jun daily 10am–6pm; Oct–Apr Wed–Mon 10am–6pm.

The Pic du Canigou (Mount Canigou) and the Parc Naturel Régional des Pyrénées Catalanes (Regional Nature Park of the Catalan Pyrénées)

The Pic du Canigou (or Puig del Canigó, to give the mountain its Catalan name) is one of the highest summits in the eastern Pyrénées. Towering to 2,785m (9,137ft), it can be seen on a clear day from the lowlands of the Aude and the Mediterranean coast. The peak marks the eastern boundary of the Parc Naturel Régional des Pyrénées Catalanes, a huge stretch of mountainous territory which runs along the Spanish border. Like other regional natural parks in France, it embraces a number of small towns, villages and farmland as well as wilderness areas, but it certainly has enough wide open spaces and big skies to satisfy anyone who wants to get well off the beaten track.

The eastern sector of the park, north of the village of Font-Romeu, offers equally splendid panoramas. It is dominated by the 2,921m (9,583ft) Pic Carlit, which is flanked to the south by an array of slightly lower peaks and to the north by an arc of natural and artificial lakes. In summer, these attract large numbers of anglers, picnickers and hikers. For those intending to walk to the top of Pic Carlit, the best starting point is the tiny hamlet of Combeleran at the southern end of Lac des Bouillouses (*14km/9 miles northwest of Mont-Louis on D60*). Allow at least eight hours to hike to the summit and back: proper walking boots and wet-weather clothing are essential. The walk is not very demanding, but only experienced walkers with good mountain skills should try it outside the warmer months of May–September. *Park headquarters, 1 rue Dagobert, Mont-Louis. Tel: (0468) 04 97 60. www.parc-pyrenees-catalanes.fr*

Font-Romeu

Font-Romeu is promoted as the leading winter sports destination in Languedoc-Roussillon, with around 30 downhill ski slopes, the highest of which start at 2,200m (7,220ft) above sea level. Most of these pistes are unchallenging, but Font-Romeu also offers a choice of other exciting winter sports, including cross-country skiing, *raquette* (snowshoeing) and dog-sledding with teams of huskies on more than 80km (50 miles) of winter trails. In summer, the resort is a convenient place to stay if you wish to explore the Parc Naturel Régional des Pyrénées Catalanes. Used as a high-altitude base for French athletes in training for the 1968 Olympic Games in Mexico City, Font-Romeu's other claim to fame is as the home of a famous medieval statue of the Virgin, which is kept for part of the year in its own chapel, the Ermitage, in Font-Romeu, and from September to Easter in the Église de Saint-Martin in Odeillo, about 3km (2 miles) from the centre of the modern resort.

Bolquère

Just outside Font-Romeu, Bolquère is the highest railway station in France, and the highest point on one of France's most dramatic scenic rail journeys, the Petit Train Jaune (Little Yellow Train), which trundles from Villefranche-de-Conflent (about 40km/ 25 miles east of Font-Romeu) through the Pyrénées-Catalanes, then across the high moors and pastures of the remote Cerdagne region to the Spanish

(*Cont. on p86*)

Pyrénées-Orientales and Corbières

The icy peaks of the Pic du Canigou in winter

Walk: Pic du Canigou ascent

Rising to 2,785m (9,137ft) above sea level, the Pic du Canigou is a prominent Pyrenean landmark. This is the least demanding route to the top, but it is still a tough hike for fit walkers, requiring proper walking boots, wet-weather clothing and a large-scale map of the massif. The best time for the walk is early autumn, as heavy snow in winter (lasting until late spring) makes the ascent difficult and risky, while heat-haze and high temperatures make it a less rewarding trip in summer.

The walk covers 10km (6¹/₄ miles) in distance and 600m (1,970ft) in altitude and should take four or five hours.

4WD taxis operate between Prades, 45km (29 miles) west of Perpignan on the N116, and the Chalet des Cortalets, where this walk begins (book taxis through the Office de Tourisme at Vernet-les-Bains. Tel: (0468) 05 55 35. www.ot.vernet-les-bains.fr).

1 Chalet des Cortalets

This mountain refuge, 2,150m (7,054ft) above sea level, is an unassuming building which served as a base for *maquisards* (guerilla fighters) of the French Resistance during World War II. *For approximately 3km (2 miles), this walk follows the route of the GR10 long-distance walking trail. The real ascent begins just beyond the refuge and is clearly signposted to Canigou, on the left (south) of the dirt track. Follow the trail as it runs south and then bears west to hug the north shore of a small lake.*

2 Lac des Cortalets

Fed by mountain streams, the lake can be dazzling blue under summer or autumn skies. Look out for marmots (and listen for their strident alarm calls) on the slopes around and above

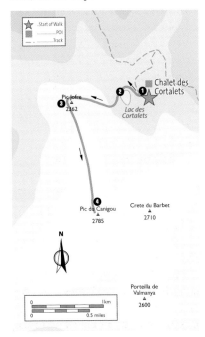

The hike is rewarded by stunning Pyrenean views

the lake. These cute, furry rodents came close to extinction in the first half of the 20th century and were reintroduced to the region in the 1950s.

Continue around the north side of the lake for around 1.6km (1 mile) to a picnic site. Right on the 2,000m (6,560ft) contour line, this is a good place for a breather and a snack before continuing northwest along the GR10 as it curves around the flank of the Pic Jofre.

3 Pic Jofre

At 2,362m (7,749ft), the Pic Jofre is dwarfed by its higher neighbour, Canigou, but is nonetheless an impressive summit.

The route to Canigou now parts company with the GR10. Where the paths diverge, turn left and follow the Canigou trail as it trends south, keeping the Pic Jofre on your left. The path now starts to climb steadily towards Canigou, dead ahead to the south. After about 2km (1¼ miles), passing a series of crags and massive boulders, you'll arrive at the foot

of the Canigou summit. The final pitch to the peak will take up to two hours. Care is needed, as the slope is steep and rocky and the path is not always easy to trace.

4 Pic du Canigou

A *table d'orientation* at the summit allows you to identify the Pyrenean peaks that are visible from Canigou, and the views are stupendous. From here, it's easy to see why Canigou is such an important symbol for the Catalan people, with the whole of Spanish and French Catalonia within sight and a panoply of small Catalan flags decorating its bare rock. On 23 June each year, Catalans light a great bonfire on the summit, and torches are carried from it to light beacons in hundreds of towns and villages throughout Catalonia.

Retrace your steps to the Chalet des Cortalets, where you should have pre-booked a 4WD taxi to take you back to Prades.

The crumbling yet atmospheric Château de Durban

frontier and the railway's western terminus at Latour-de-Carole, where it connects with the main SNCF French railway network and with the RENFE Spanish railway system. The first section of this historic scenic railway opened in 1903 and it was finally completed in 1927, becoming the highest rail line in France.

Gare de Bolquère-Eune, 3km (2 miles) east of Font-Romeu.

Château de Durban

Crowning its hilltop above the medieval village of Durban-Corbières, the Château de Durban shows its age more than most of the evocative castle ruins of Languedoc-Roussillon. Built in the 11th century, it must once have been one of the grandest noble seats in the region, with splendid Renaissance windows and ornate carved stonework.

Now all that survives is the north wall and two dilapidated towers. Despite this, the hilltop fortress is still a striking building. In the late 19th century, its last aristocratic owner sold the crumbling castle to a local mason, who demolished most of the building to re-use its stones – hence its rather woeful present-day condition.

Durban-Corbières.
www.contree-durban-corbieres.com.
Open: 24 hours. Free admission.

Tautavel

Tautavel is an unassuming farming village in the foothills of the Fenouillèdes. In 1971, an amazing discovery propelled it to fame, when archaeologists unearthed parts of a skull belonging to *Homo erectus*, indicating that these pre-modern humans lived here as early as 500,000 years BC.

Centre Européen de Préhistoire (European Centre of Prehistory)

Pride of place in this fine museum goes to a reconstruction of the unbelievably ancient skull of *Homo erectus*, found in a cave at the Caune d'Arago, near Tautavel. Painstaking excavations revealed more than 250,000 stone and bone implements, animal remains and other evidence of the earliest European settlement ever discovered.

Avenue Léon Jean Grégory Tautavel. Tel: (0468) 29 07 76. www.tautavel.com. Open: Jan–Mar & Oct–Dec daily 10am–12.30pm & 2–5pm; Apr–Jun daily 10am–12.30pm & 2–6pm; Jul & Aug daily 10am–7pm. Admission charge.

Les Premiers Habitants de l'Europe (The First Inhabitants of Europe)

This stunning modern museum plunges deep into prehistory, with a collection of more than 300 remarkable relics of early humankind in Europe, dating from more than 800,000 years ago. The tools, fossils and other finds come from archaeological sites from France, Spain and Georgia.

Palais des Congrès, Tautavel. Tel: (0468) 29 07 76. www.tautavel.com. Open: Jan–Mar & Oct–Dec daily 11.30am–1pm & 2.30–5.30pm; Apr–Jun & Sept daily 11.30am–1pm & 2.30–6.30pm; Jul & Aug daily 11.30am–7.30pm. Admission charge.

Château d'Arques

This graceful little castle is less forbidding and grim-looking than many of its contemporaries. It has four round towers, linked by curtain walls, built of pale-pink stone and capped by pagoda-like pantiled roofs. The château was built in 1316 by the grandson of one of Simon de Montfort's crusading knights.

Arques on D613. Tel: (0468) 69 82 87. www.chateau-arques.fr

Dinosauria: Le Musée des Dinosaures d'Espéraza (Espéraza Dinosaur Museum)

The limestone sedimentary rocks of Languedoc-Roussillon have yielded numerous dinosaur fossils from the Cretaceous era, 70 million years ago, when the region had a tropical climate. Dinosauria boasts one of the largest collections of dinosaur skeletons in Europe, including terrifying

Tour Magdala in Rennes-le-Château

Pyrénées-Orientales and Corbières

The ancient fortress of Villefranche-de-Conflent

reconstructions of Tyrannosaurus rex, the huge 22m (72ft) Mamenchisaurus, and the largest winged dinosaur ever found, Quetzalcoatlus. Seeing the remains of these enormous creatures makes them real in a way that no digital reconstruction ever can.

Espéraza, 4km (2½ miles) west of Couiza on the D118. Tel: (0468) 74 26 88. www.dinosauria.org. Open: mid-Feb– end Jun & Sept–late Nov & 26 Dec–mid- Jan daily 10.30am–12.30pm; Jul & Aug daily 10am–7pm. Closed: mid-Jan–mid- Feb. Admission charge.

Rennes-le-Château

The hilltop village of Rennes-le- Château, above the upper reaches of the Aude valley, has become one of Languedoc-Roussillon's most-visited locations thanks to a 'legend' which arose to explain the apparent wealth and unusually comfortable lifestyle of its village priest, François Bérenger Saunière (1852–1917), during the late 19th century (*see below*).

3.5km (2 miles) south of Couiza.

Domaine Bérenger Saunière

In the 1890s, Bérenger Saunière had his church expensively renovated, added a neo-Gothic tower, the Tour Magdala, as well as an orangerie and the rather lavish Villa Bethania, where he lived with Marie Denarnaud, who was his 'housekeeper' for most of his life. Naturally, people wondered how Saunière raised the money for all this. There were rumours that he had discovered a hidden treasure trove, perhaps concealed in the church by Visigoths or Merovingian kings, by the crusading Templar order or by the mythical Priory of Zion. It was even suggested that he had discovered the Holy Grail.

The truth seems to be rather more mundane: Saunière appears to have had a lucrative sideline peddling mail-order prayers, masses or blessings all over France in return for 'charitable donations' to his church, some of which he used to improve his own quarters. As a result, he was defrocked by the Catholic Church, but defiantly continued to hold Mass in his own chapel until his death. Marie Denardaud lived on until 1953, and for the rest of her life tantalised villagers and visitors with hints that Saunière really had discovered an ancient treasure hoard. In the 1950s the legend was taken up and embellished by local entrepreneurs who were keen to attract curious sightseers to the village. In 1982, authors Henry Lincoln, Michael Bagent and Richard Leigh published *The Holy Blood and the Holy Grail*, which claimed that Rennes-le-Château held clues to a remarkable secret – that Jesus, instead of dying on the cross, survived and fathered children with Mary Magdalene, and that his descendants founded the Frankish Merovingian dynasty. The book raised the profile of Rennes-le-Château still further. In 2003, Dan Brown's novel *The Da Vinci Code* also referred to the supposed 'mystery' of the chapel, with

the result that visitor numbers jumped from 80,000 in 2004 to a peak of 112,000 in 2007 – the film version was released in 2006. By 2009 the number of visitors had dropped back to a mere 97,000.

The visit to the Domaine Bérenger Saunière comprises the original medieval *presbytère* (chapel), the Villa Bethania (Saunière's comfortable residence), the oratory, Tour Magdala and the orangery. The chapel is crammed with wooden statues and carvings of saints and angels, into which conspiracy theorist have read a multitude of meanings. In fact, Saunière bought the whole lot, ready-made, from one of the many manufacturers who specialised in run-of-the-mill church furnishings.

Note that from the beginning of July to the end of August, Rennes-le-Château is pedestrian-only, and a 'mini-train' carries visitors from the main

(*Cont. on p92*)

The precariously poised Château Peyrepertuse

Tour: Le Train Jaune (The Yellow Train)

The scenery along this historic railway changes dramatically, following the upper Têt valley from the foothills of the Canigou massif through steep gorges, then to the moorland plateau country of the Cerdagne, with the Pyrénées always in sight to the south.

It takes two and a half hours to travel the 63km (40 miles) of the route without disembarking.

Start at the eastern end of the route, Villefranche-de-Conflent (May–Sept up to six departures daily, from 8.30am).

1 Villefranche-de-Conflent

Before boarding the Train Jaune, take time to explore this old fortress town. Conquered by Louis XIV's troops in 1654 after a siege lasting eight days, Villefranche's defences were strengthened by Louis' great military architect, Vauban, to defend France against Spain. They are still remarkably impressive – so impressive, in fact, that the Spanish never attempted to breach them.

From Villefranche, the line follows the upper Têt valley, skirting the northern flank of the Canigou massif, passes through the small village of Serdinya and, after about 8km (5 miles), arrives at Olette, 607m (1,991ft) above sea level.

2 Olette

The twin towers of a medieval castle stand above an age-old village that seems to be on the verge of tumbling into the steep valley of the Têt.

The line continues along the south side of the Têt for about 6km (4 miles).

3 Thuès-Carança

This is the station for the somnolent little spa town of Thuès-les-Bains and, more excitingly, for the Gorges de Carança and some spectacular canyon hiking on trails, bridges and walkways.

Leaving Thuès-Carança, the train crosses the mouth of the gorge, then passes through it, allowing passengers a glimpse of the spectacular cliffs on either side. After 8km (5 miles), climbing to 1,373m (4,504ft) and passing through Fontpedrouse and Planes, it crosses another dramatic bridge.

4 Pont Gisclard

This bridge is a triumph of early 20th-century railway engineering. Carrying the line over the 80m (260ft) river gorge, it has a total length of 234m (768ft). Completed in 1908, it was the first bridge of its kind to be built in France.

2km (1¼ miles) west of the bridge, the line arrives at Mont-Louis, 1,510m (4,954ft) above sea level.

5 Mont-Louis

Mont-Louis' historic centre is dominated by star-shaped fortifications that bear the unmistakable stamp of Vauban, and it is still garrisoned by the French army, which uses the nearby mountains for special forces training.

6km (4 miles) west of Mont-Louis, the Train Jaune reaches its highest point.

6 Bolquère-Eune

Bolquère is the highest railway station in France, and at 1,593m (5,226ft) it is

the highest point on this scenic rail journey. It's only 2km (1¼ miles) from Font-Romeu, Languedoc-Roussillon's top winter sports resort.

From here, the Petit Train Jaune winds southwest for 16km (10 miles) across the high, treeless moorland and sheep pastures of the remote Cerdagne region, through Bourg-Madame to Latour-de-Carole on the Franco-Spanish border.

7 Latour-de-Carole

In one sense, this mountainous terminus is the end of the line – but only for the Train Jaune, which connects here with two national rail networks.

From here, you can link up with SNCF trains to take you down to Carcassonne, or RENFE trains to Barcelona.

Tour: Le Train Jaune (The Yellow Train)

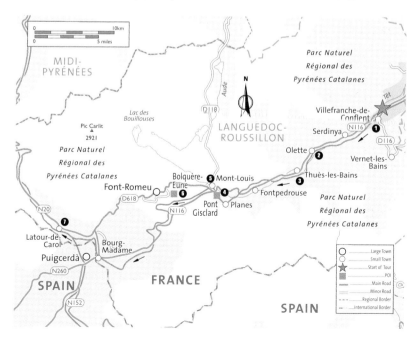

village car park to the Belvedere, the highest point of the village.

Domaine Bérenger Saunière, Rennes-le-Château. Tel: (0468) 31 38 85. www.rennes-le-chateau.fr. Open: Jul–mid-Sept & mid-Oct–end Oct daily 10am–7.15pm; mid–end Sept, May & Jun daily 10am–6.15pm; end Sept–mid-Oct daily 10am–5.45pm; Nov–Apr daily 10am–1pm & 2–5.15pm. Admission charge.

Château de Puilaurens

Puilaurens was once the most formidable border stronghold on France's frontier with the Spanish Kingdom of Aragon. On its impregnable pinnacle, 700m (2,296ft) above the little village of Lapradelle-Puilaurens, it is still an impressive sight, with its round tower and curtain walls occupying the whole top of the rocky crag, and the views from the ramparts are breathtaking – as is the steep climb to the castle. The first castle here was built in 985, and it withstood a number of assaults by Aragonese and Spanish forces during France's centuries-long border wars. With the Treaty of the Pyrénées in 1659, it became redundant, but it was still garrisoned until the French Revolution, when it was finally abandoned.

Lapradelle-Puilaurens. Tel: (0468) 20 65 26. www.payscathare.org. Open: Feb–Apr & Oct–mid-Nov daily 10am–5pm; March Sat & Sun 10am–5pm; Jun & Sept daily 10am–7pm; Jul & Aug daily 9am–8pm. Admission charge.

The ruins of Château de Quéribus provide commanding views

Grotte L'Aguzou (L'Aguzou Cave)

Unlike many of the caves which plunge deep into the limestone rock of Languedoc-Roussillon, L'Aguzou has been kept in a virtually pristine state, so a visit to this complex of caverns feels like a real adventure. Visitors don overalls and safety helmets equipped with electric headlamps before setting out on an eight-hour journey into the bowels of the earth, taking them through vaulted grottos adorned with glittering crystal formations, stalactites and limestone pinnacles.

15km (9 miles) north of Axat on the D118. Tel: (0468) 20 45 38. http://grotte.aguzou.pagesperso-orange.fr. Tours (book in advance) in groups of 8–10 people begin at 9am year-round. Equipment provided. Admission charge.

Château de Peyrepertuse

Peyrepertuse is best seen in early morning, when the sun lends a rosy glow to the cliffs on which the upper castle stands, appearing to grow straight out of the living rock. Like many of the royal strongholds dotted around the hills of the Fenouillèdes and the southern Corbières, the château was a lynchpin of France's medieval frontier defences. The earliest stronghold, the *château bas* (lower castle), dates from the 11th century, while the *château supérieur* (upper castle), also known as San Jordi (Saint George), was built in the second half of the 13th century. Despite its apparent size, the castle had only a small garrison of around 15 men-at-arms, and it was never besieged. It was manned until the late 18th century, when its last garrison was withdrawn after the Revolution.

Duilhac. Tel: (0671) 58 63 36. www.chateau-peyrepertuse.com. Open: Feb, Mar, Nov & Dec daily 10am–5pm; Apr, May & Oct daily 10am–6.30pm; Jun & Sept daily 9am–7pm; Jul & Aug daily 9am–8.30pm. Admission charge.

Château de Quéribus

Like many of the so-called Cathar castles, Château de Quéribus perches on a near-unassailable pinnacle, 728m (2,388ft) above sea level. From its battlements there are outstanding views southward to the peaks of the Pyrénées and east to the Mediterranean coast. Built in the late 10th century by the Counts of Barcelona, it was one of the last Cathar holdouts until it finally fell into the hands of Louis IX of France in 1255 after the local lord, Chabert de Barbaira, surrendered to the king and yielded Quéribus and other strongholds as a token of good faith. Today, it is little more than a hollow shell, but is worth visiting just for the view.

5km (3 miles) north of the D117, signposted from Maury. Tel: (0468) 45 03 69. www.cucugnan.fr. Open: Jan, Nov & Dec daily 10am–5pm; Feb daily 9am–5.30pm; Mar daily 10am–6pm; Apr–Jun & Sept daily 9.30am–7pm; Jul, Aug & Oct daily 9am–8pm. Admission charge.

Carcassonne and the Aude valley

Embracing a vast expanse of rolling vineyards and hidden glens, where ruined Cathar castles stand above quaint villages, this is one of the most varied regions of Languedoc-Roussillon. Its character is shaped by the Aude, which begins as a fast-flowing Pyrenean stream and grows into a fully-fledged river with stretches of white water, then slows as it approaches Carcassonne.

Here the river turns east to meander its way to the Mediterranean, watering the vineyards of the Minervois and Aude wine regions along the way. Parallel to the Aude runs one of the extraordinary engineering feats of the 17th century, the Canal du Midi, while north of Carcassonne the forested hills of the Montagne Noire rise to the 1,211m (3,973ft)-high summit of the Pic de Nore. The prosperous lowlands are dotted with small market towns and farming villages, but the hills are more sparsely populated and are criss-crossed with hiking and riding trails. The Montagne Noire's thick forests of Spanish chestnut, conifers and holm oak provide refuge for an abundance of wildlife, including wild boar, roe deer, pine martens, red squirrels and badgers, as well as an array of gorgeous butterflies and birds, including some rare migrant species. Amid all this natural beauty, Carcassonne's medieval

Carcassonne's world-renowned ramparts

city is the best-known, most spectacular and most visited tourism destination in Languedoc-Roussillon.

CARCASSONNE
Cité Médiévale

The bastions and ramparts of Carcassonne's medieval fortress city are the single most recognisable landmark of Languedoc-Roussillon and attract hundreds of thousands of visitors each year. The Cité Médiévale is a UNESCO World Heritage Site. It certainly looks authentically archaic (and has been the backdrop for numerous films, including Luc Besson's *Jeanne d'Arc* and Kevin Costner's *Robin Hood: Prince of Thieves*) but appearances are deceptive. It owes much of its present appearance to the

architect Eugène Viollet-le-Duc, who used a great deal of imagination and artistic licence when he took charge of the Cité's restoration during the 19th century. The 3km (2-mile) ring of ramparts is studded with more than 50 towers and barbicans, each capped with a distinctive conical roof (one of Viollet-le-Duc's inventive touches). Within, the medieval streets are crammed with cafés, restaurants, souvenir shops and galleries, as well as several hotels.

Cité Médiévale Office de Tourisme, Tour Ouest, Porte de Narbonne.
Tel: (0468) 10 24 36.
www.carcassonnetourisme.com.
Open: Jul & Aug Mon–Sat 9am–7pm, Sun 9am–1pm; rest of the year Mon–Sat 9am–6pm, Sun 9am–1pm.

Basilique Saint-Nazaire et Saint-Celse

Founded in the early 9th century, this splendid Gothic church was consecrated in 1096 and completed in the early 12th century. Like so much else in the Cité, it was restored and remodelled in the late 19th century by Viollet-le-Duc. Outside, grotesque gargoyles peer from the roofline. Inside are some outstanding stone carvings dating from the 14th century, and a huge pipe organ which is used for concerts in summer.

Place Saint-Nazaire. Open: Mon–Sat 9–11.45am & 1.45–6pm, Sun 9–10.45am & 1.45–6pm, Sun Mass 11am.
Free admission.

Château Comtal
(Castle of the Viscounts)

The castle of the Trencavel Viscounts of Carcassonne, with its cavernous halls and sturdy walls, is the most impressive part of the Cité Médiévale. The castle houses a collection of antique stonework and other medieval relics, and an audiovisual presentation brings its fascinating history vividly to life, from its 12th-century foundation to its restoration by Viollet-le-Duc. The admission price includes a guided tour of the ramparts as well as the tour of the castle.

1 rue Viollet-le-Duc. Tel: (0468) 11 70 70. www.monuments-nationaux.fr. Open for guided tours only: Oct–Mar daily 9.30am–5pm; Apr–Sept daily 9.30am–6.30pm. Admission charge (EU citizens under 26 free).

Memoires du Moyen Age
(Memories of the Middle Ages)

This small museum re-creates the history of the Cité, from its earliest beginnings as a Roman fortress in the 3rd century through the Cathar wars and the turbulent Middle Ages. Outside stands a re-creation of a *bricole*, a massive, stone-hurling catapult which was used to bombard castles like Carcassonne in the sieges of the 13th century.

40 chemin des Anglais.
Tel: (0468) 71 08 65. Open: 10am–7pm.
Admission charge.

Musée de la Chevalerie
(Museum of Chivalry)

Battle-axes, bows and broadswords from the Middle Ages, costumes, armour, textiles and tapestries are on show here, along with film props such as the bow

The Gothic Basilique Saint-Nazaire et Saint-Celse

used by Kevin Costner in *Robin Hood: Prince of Thieves*.

2 porte d'Aude. Tel: (0468) 72 75 51. www.musee-chevalerie.com. Open: Apr–Jun, Sept & Oct daily 10am–1pm & 3–7pm; Jul & Aug daily 10am–9pm. Admission charge.

Bastide de Saint-Louis (Ville Basse)

On the opposite bank of the Aude river from the Cité Médiévale, Carcassonne's Ville Basse (Lower Town), also known as the Bastide de Saint-Louis, is less self-consciously picturesque than the old citadel, but it is a pleasantly relaxed place, with a few sights worth seeing. Laid out on a grid pattern, it centres on Place Carnot, a main square lined with cafés where the colourful produce market takes place several mornings a week. The main shopping street, Rue Clemenceau, is pedestrianised. The Aude flows round the southeast side of the city, crossed by two bridges – the 14th-century Pont Vieux and the modern Pont Neuf – while the Canal du Midi forms its northern boundary.

Carcassonne Central Office de Tourisme, 28 rue de Verdun. Tel: (0468) 10 24 30. www.carcassonnetourisme.com. Open: Jul & Aug Mon–Sat 9am–7pm, Sun 9am–1pm; rest of the year Mon–Sat 9am–6pm, Sun 9am–1pm.

Cathédrale Saint-Michel

This 13th-century southern Gothic church with its barrel-vaulted nave surrounded by 12 chapels has an octagonal tower which is the most prominent and distinctive landmark of the Ville Basse. Inside is a remarkable collection of religious works of art and architecture.

Rue Voltaire. Open: Mon–Sat 9am–11.45am & 1.45–6pm, Sun 9–10.45am & 1.45–6pm, Sun Mass 11am. Free admission.

Chapelle des Jésuites (Jesuit Chapel)

Part of the city's Jesuit college, this Baroque chapel was restored to its former glory in 2000 after many years of lying derelict. Entrance is through a gracious 18th-century gateway; within are coffered painted ceilings and an impressive reredos. The chapel is worth a look just for its architecture, but it also serves as a venue for a changing programme of art exhibitions and performances of classical and religious music.

Rue des Études. Tel: (0468) 72 69 94. Open: Mon–Sat 10am–noon & 3–6pm. Free admission.

Église Saint-Vincent

Carcassonne's most prominent church towers over the Ville Basse. Inside, its Gothic nave is one of the widest and longest in Languedoc-Roussillon, and the 54m (177ft) steeple, which has a carillon of more than 50 bells, can be seen from all around the city.

Corner of Rue 4 Septembre and Rue Torney. Open: Mon–Sat 9–11.45am & 1.45–6pm, Sun 9–10.45am & 1.45–6pm, Sun Mass 11am. Free admission.

Walk: Around the Cité Médiévale

This walk takes in the high points of Languedoc-Roussillon's best-known landmark and tourism icon, the walled medieval citadel of Carcassonne.

Allow two or three hours, including an hour for the guided visit to the Château Comtal and a leisurely walk around the Cité's 3km (2-mile) ring of ramparts.

Start at Notre Dame de la Santé, at the west end of the Pont Vieux.

1 Pont Vieux (Old Bridge)

The Pont Vieux crosses the Aude from the Ville Basse (Lower Town, also called Bastide de Saint-Louis),

which was built on the orders of Louis IX in the mid-13th century, and affords views of the spectacular citadel on its hill on the east bank of the river.

At the east end of the bridge, turn right on to Rue de la Barbacane, then after

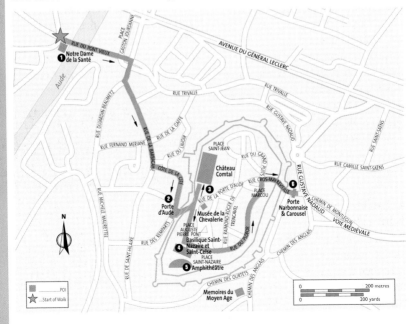

around 400m (435yds) turn left and ascend the zigzag cobbled lane to Porte d'Aude. It's a stiff walk up to the ramparts from the riverside, but well worth it in order to appreciate the formidable defences.

2 Porte d'Aude (Aude Gate)

Turn around to admire the view of the lower city from this arched gateway in the towering walls of the citadel.

Enter the Cité Médiévale through the Porte d'Aude, and turn left along Rue de la Porte d'Aude. Turn left across Place du Château to enter the castle.

3 Château Comtal

The vast castle of the counts was the seat of the Trencavel dynasty, who were vassals of the counts of Toulouse, from the mid-12th century until 1229, when King Louis IX asserted royal control.

Allow an hour for the guided visit to the castle and the video presentation which explains its history and its reconstruction during the 19th century.

Return to Rue de la Porte d'Aude, then turn left on Rue du Four Saint-Nazaire and follow it to Place Auguste Pierre Pont.

4 Basilique Saint-Nazaire et Saint-Celse

In front of you now is the impressive Gothic basilica (see p95), originally constructed in the 10th century.

Walk round the basilica to Place Saint-Nazaire.

5 Amphithéâtre

Immediately south of the basilica is the amphitheatre, which looks like a Roman relic but in fact was constructed in 1908. It provides a venue for all sorts of outdoor performances.

From the east side of Place Saint-Nazaire, walk along Rue du Plofor to Place Marcou, which is a good spot to pause for refreshment. Turn right on Rue Cros-Mayrevieille, which leads to the Porte Narbonnaise.

6 Porte Narbonnaise (Narbonne Gate)

Along with the Porte d'Aude, this gate is the city's other main access point. Just outside it, in summer, you'll find a picturesque old-fashioned carousel whose painted horses and other mounts will delight children.

From the car park opposite the Porte Narbonnaise, catch the navette (mini-shuttle) which takes you back to the centre of the Halte Centrale du Dôme in the lower town.

Towers of the Porte Narbonnaise

Distinctive conical turret at Carcassonne

Les Halles (Covered Market)

Carcassonne's 18th-century covered market was restored in 2007 and is now used for art exhibitions as well as occasionally providing market space for more than 20 butchers, grocers, fishmongers and other produce merchants.

Rue Aimé-Ramond & Rue Verdun. Open: Mon–Fri 9am–4pm, Sat 8am–noon. Free admission.

Musée des Beaux-Arts (Fine Arts Museum)

The museum's rooms, full of its run-of-the-mill permanent collection of 18th- and 19th-century landscape paintings, are not a bad place to spend an hour or so on a hot afternoon or wet day, but its occasional visiting exhibitions are usually very interesting.

Rue Verdun. Tel: (0468) 77 73 70. www.carcassonne.org. Open: Jun–Sept Wed–Sun 10am–6pm; Oct–May Tue–Sat 10am–noon & 2–6pm. Free admission.

Port de Carcassonne (Carcassonne River Port)

The Canal du Midi broadens into the Port de Carcassonne between the town's railway station and the Ville Basse. In summer, it bustles with canal boats, cruisers and yachts, and several companies offer day trips with a multilingual commentary describing the history of the canal and the workings of its locks, such as **Carcassonne Croisières** (*Promenade du Canal. Tel: (0468) 71 61 26. www.carcassonne-croisiere.com*).

Lac de la Cavayère (Cavayère Lake)

Just outside Carcassonne, this artificial lake is the city's 'seaside', with swimming beaches (with lifeguards on duty in summer), canoes and pedalos for hire, snack bar and restaurant. It is a very pleasant place to spend a hot summer afternoon.

Cavayère, Chemin des Bartavelles, 1km (just over ½ mile) south of the Cité Médiévale. Open: dawn–dusk. Free admission.

Le Parc Australien (Australian Park)

Kangaroos, wallabies, possums and other Australian wildlife are the main attraction at this park just outside

Carcassonne. There are also animals from other continents, including camels and a flock of ostriches, which are raised here for their meat and eggs. Ostrich plumes, egg shells and delicious ostrich steaks (great for barbecues) are sold in the park shop.

Chemin des Bartavelles.
Tel: (0434) 42 88 07.
http://leparcaustralien.free.fr.
Open: May–Sept daily 10.30am–6.30pm; Oct Wed & Sat 2–5pm, Sun 10.30am–5pm; winter opening times vary, see website. Admission charge.

OUTSIDE CARCASSONNE
Castelnaudary and the Canal du Midi

Set in the rolling farmland of the Pays Lauragais, the small town of Castelnaudary is one of the most important ports along the Canal du

The verdant Canal du Midi

CASSOULET CENTRAL

Castelnaudary proudly claims to be the capital of *cassoulet* (the savoury casserole of pork, sausage, duck, goose and white beans), which is the trademark dish of southwest France, and which appears on all the town's restaurant menus. It can also be bought in tins, so it is a handy standby for those planning a self-catering canal cruise. Castelnaudary's Fête du Cassoulet, which celebrates this culinary favourite, takes place on the last weekend of August, with music, dancing, a market packed with regional delicacies, and *cassoulet* for breakfast, lunch and dinner.

Midi. Its Grand Bassin, bustling with narrowboats and cruisers all summer, is a popular starting point for boat trips along the canal. Two historic churches – the 16th-century Chapelle Notre-Dame-de-Pitié and the 13th-century Collégiale Saint-Michel – overlook the town centre, and guided visits can be arranged at the tourist office, which also offers multilingual guided tours of the town and nearby points of interest.

Office de Tourisme, Halle du Verdun.
Tel: (0468) 23 05 73.
www.castelnaudary-tourisme.com.
Open: Jan–Mar & Oct–Dec Mon–Fri 9am–noon & 2–5pm, Sat 9am–noon; Apr–Jun Mon–Sat 9am–noon & 2–6pm; Jul–end Sept daily 9am–1pm & 2–7pm.

Musée du Lauragais
(Lauragais Museum)

This historic building, dating from the 12th century when it was built as a courthouse and prison, now houses an

(Cont. on p104)

The Cathars

The Cathar cult flourished in Languedoc in the 12th and 13th centuries and still fascinates visitors and historians. The turbulent times of the Cathars provide a backdrop for a bevy of historical novels, such as Kate Mosse's *Labyrinth*, as well as providing material for a vast body of imaginative conspiracy theories, poorly researched 'histories' and legends that claim to have their roots in the deep medieval past but which mostly turn out to have been invented much more recently – sometimes by enterprising locals with a vested interest in promoting tourism to the region.

Regarded as heretics by the Roman Catholic Church, the Cathar *parfaits* ('perfect ones') preached an idiosyncratic doctrine based on the struggle between good and evil, and their ascetic lifestyle attracted many Christians who disliked the luxurious ways of Catholic clerics.

It also attracted less idealistic, more pragmatic supporters. The Counts of Toulouse and Carcassonne and many other powerful nobles of Languedoc realised that the Cathars could be useful supporters in their own struggle to maintain independence from the French crown, and became protectors of the Cathar religion against the papacy and its ally, the Kingdom of France.

Where the Cathars got their heretical beliefs from is still a puzzle, but some historians believe that they may have been influenced by religious ideas brought back from the Middle East by returning Crusaders who had encountered the dualistic Manichean philosophy. Born of ancient Persian beliefs, the Manichean creed, like Catharism, is based on an unending conflict between good and evil.

Catharism spread across much of France, but Languedoc, Albi, Carcassonne and Toulouse were always its heartlands. In 1209, Pope Innocent III launched the Albigensian

Lastours was a Cathar stronghold

The ramparts of Puilaurens were an intimidating sight for the Cathars' enemies

Crusade, a military campaign spearheaded by northern French soldiers of fortune and led by a French knight, Simon de Montfort. It began with the siege and sack of Béziers (and the massacre of its inhabitants) in 1209 and ended almost half a century later, with the surrender of the last Cathar strongholds to the armies of King Louis IX.

Looking at the hilltop castles that the Cathars built to resist the invaders, it's easy to see why the campaign to wipe them out took so long. Carcassonne's formidable ramparts resisted assault until its viscount negotiated a surrender. Not far north of the city, the towers of Lastours, perched atop their steep-sided crags, must have been an intimidating sight for any besieging soldier, and the giddy eyries of Peyrepertuse and Quéribus look completely unassailable.

In the end, however, they all fell. Montségur held out against the French royal forces until 1244, when its defenders were massacred to a man. Puilaurens and Quéribus surrendered in 1256. Simon de Montfort did not live to see the final defeat of the Cathar cause – he was killed by a catapult shot at the siege of Toulouse in 1218.

After the military defeat of the Cathars, the papacy sent in the Inquisition to root out any remaining Cathar believers. Hundreds were tortured or burned at the stake, while many others survived by abandoning their beliefs and returning to the Catholic faith. A few isolated Cathar communities survived until the 14th century, and one of them, Montaillou, provides the source for Emmanuel Le Roy Ladurie's remarkable history, *Montaillou*. Based on the painstaking accounts recorded by the inquisitors as they cross-examined these last Cathars, it is a fascinating insight into their lives and times.

The River Aude passes serenely through Limoux

exhibition which reveals the history of a remarkable feat of engineering, the Canal du Midi.

10 rue du Présidial. Open: Jun–Aug Tue–Sat 10am–12.30pm & 3–6.45pm, Sun 3–6.30pm; rest of the year by arrangement with the tourist office. Closed: Mon. Free admission.

Limoux

The picturesque small town of Limoux, straddling the Aude river, is today best known for its Blanquette de Limoux, which is claimed to be the world's oldest sparkling wine. Made from a blend of Chenin, Chardonnay and Mauzac grapes (which are grown in profusion in the vineyards around Limoux), it's a very acceptable and affordable alternative to Champagne. Limoux is also famed for another local speciality: nougat. This tasty treat can be bought at a number of sweet shops and delicatessens in town. The heart of the town is Place de la République, which is surrounded on three sides by arcades, while the historic centre is a labyrinth of lanes along which stand gracious 17th- and 18th-century mansions built around arcaded courtyards.

24km (15 miles) south of Carcassonne on the D118. Service Tourisme, Avenue du Pont de France. Tel: (0468) 31 11 82. www.limoux.fr

Catharama

This half-hour, multilingual audio-visual presentation sheds some light on the lost history of the Cathars, their mysterious faith and their tragic end at the hands of the Inquisition.

Tel: (0468) 31 15 89. www.d-av.com. Open: Jul & Aug Wed–Mon 2–6pm. Admission charge.

Musée des Automates (Animatronics Museum)

This magical private museum of animated, fairy-tale characters will delight younger visitors (though very small children may find the medieval characters a bit scary).
2 rue Anne-Marie Javouhey.
Tel: 0670 39 01 74. www.limoux.fr.
Open: daily 10am–12.30pm & 2–5pm.
Admission charge.

Musée Petiet (Petiet Museum)

Housed in the 19th-century family home of the local artist Marie Petiet, this museum's interesting and varied collection includes Petiet's own works, some attractive Orientalist paintings, Impressionist works, and paintings by another locally born painter, the *pointilliste* Achille Lauge.
Promenade du Tivoli. Tel: (0468) 31 85 03.
www.limoux.fr. Open: Jul & Aug Tue–Fri
9am–noon & 2–6pm, Sat 10am–noon
& 2–5pm. Closed: Sun & Mon.
Admission charge.

Lastours

Standing on a steep hilltop above the Orbiel valley, the four castle-towers of Lastours – Cabaret, Tour Régine, Surdespine and Quertinheux – are remarkable examples of medieval military architecture. Cabaret, the oldest, dates from the 11th century,
(Cont. on p108)

The historic town centre of Limoux

Drive: The Upper Aude

The scenery of the Aude valley, south of Carcassonne, is dramatically different from that of the vine-covered lowlands around the city. This drive passes through attractive medieval towns and pauses at viewpoints with impressive panomaras and at age-old abbeys and châteaux.

Allow eight hours, including stops, to cover the 130km (81-mile) drive.

Leave Carcassonne by the D118 and drive 24km (15 miles) south to Limoux.

1 Limoux

This small medieval town (*see pp104–5*) with its arcaded central square is a pleasant first stop, and several of its wineries offer guided visits and free sampling of their *brut* (dry) and *doux* (sweet) sparkling wines. A visit to the Catharama exhibition provides an enjoyable introduction to the fascinating history of the Cathars, whose hilltop strongholds are dotted around the region.
Continue south on the D118 for 8km (5 miles) to Alet-les-Bains.

2 Alet-les-Bains

Alet-les-Bains is named for its thermal springs, which have been renowned for their supposed therapeutic properties since Roman times. The town square, surrounded by half-timbered houses, does not seem to have changed much since medieval times.

Continue south on D118 for 8km (5 miles) to Couiza. From here, turn left, following signposts, up a steeply winding minor road for 3.5km (2 miles).

3 Rennes-le-Château

Rennes-le-Château's extravagantly decorated church (*see p88*) has become the centre of a plethora of mysteries and historical conspiracy theories. Its parish priest, Bérenger Saunière, was rumoured to have discovered hidden Cathar treasure. Later theorists have claimed to discover coded messages in the church's carved saints and demons.
Return to Couiza and turn east, following the D613 for 10km (6 miles) to the Donjon d'Arques.

4 Château d'Arques

The massive square tower of this 13th–14th-century castle looms just to the left of the road. Round towers buttress each corner of the 25m (82ft) keep, and inside, dramatically soaring Gothic vaults support its great halls,

which are lit by tall arched windows.
*Continue eastward for 6km (3¾ miles)
to enter the Col du Paradis.*

5 Col du Paradis

This serpentine mountain pass is one of
the most breathtaking parts of the
route. Before you ascend the col, pause
at the (clearly signposted) viewpoint
south of the road to enjoy the
panoramic view south to the 1,230m
(4,035ft) Pic de Bugarach and the
foothills of the Pyrénées.
*Carry on for 20.5km (13 miles) through
Mouthoumet to Villerouge-Termenès.*

6 Villerouge-Termenès

This village, founded in the 12th
century, is notorious as the spot where
Bélibaste, the last of the Cathar *parfaits*
('perfect ones'), was burned at the stake
in 1321. The 12th-century Église Saint-
Étienne and a 12th–14th-century
château are relics of the turbulent times
of the Cathars.
*Follow the D613 east for 4.5km (3 miles),
then turn left on the D23 to Lagrasse.*

7 Lagrasse

Lagrasse is undoubtedly one of the
most striking of the region's walled
medieval villages, with cobbled streets,
a 14th-century covered market, and an
abbey founded in the 8th century by
the Frankish emperor Charlemagne.
*Turn left on to the D3 and follow it for
30km (19 miles) to Trèbes. Turn left on
to the D303 to return to Carcassonne.*

Drive: The Upper Aude

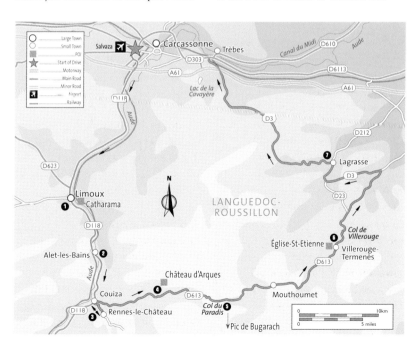

while Surdespine was built a century later. Their lord, Pierre-Roger Cabaret, defended them against the anti-Cathar crusaders led by Simon de Montfort until he finally surrendered in 1211. Tour Régine and Quertinheux are later additions, built in the 14th century. All four are now in ruins and are arguably more impressive from a distance than from close up. A viewpoint (signposted 'Belvédère' from Lastours village) is accessible by car and offers a great panorama of all four of the ruined towers. Energetic visitors can climb a steep pathway to the hilltop on which the castles stand, but there is also a great view of two of the ruined towers from the main street in Lastours. Even more evocative is the *son et lumière* show which takes place every week in summer, when the castles are lit up and their history is recounted to a musical accompaniment (*Tel: (0468) 77 56 01. www.lastorresdecabaret.overblog.com. Open: Jul–mid-Aug Tue 10.15pm. Admission charge*). Lastours also has a *café-boulangerie* (which sells cold drinks, coffee, pastries and sandwiches as well as bread), two small restaurants and a handful of places to stay.
Châteaux de Lastours, 15km (9 miles) north of Carcassonne. Tel: (0468) 77 56 02. http://les4chateaux-lastours.lwdsoftware. net. Open: Feb, Mar, Nov & Dec Sat & Sun 10am–5pm; Apr–Jun & Sept daily 10am–6pm; Jul & Aug daily 9am–8pm; Oct daily 10am–5pm. Closed: Jan. Admission charge.

Caunes-Minervois

Caunes-Minervois is famous for its quarries, which produce a rich red marble which, since the 17th century, has been used to adorn some of France's grandest buildings, including the Trianon palace at Versailles and the Arc de Triomphe in Paris. Set between the vineyards of the Minervois and the foothills of the Montagne Noire, this is one of the region's prettiest villages, and at its heart is an impressive abbey, built on the site of a 7th-century church.
16km (10 miles) northeast of Carcassonne on the D620. Office de Tourisme du Haut-Minervois, Ruelle du Monestier, Caunes-Minervois.

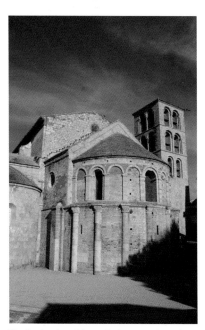

The fascinating Abbaye de Caunes-Minervois

Tel: (0468) 76 34 74. Email:
officedetourisme@hautminervois.fr

Abbaye de Caunes-Minervois
The abbey embraces some ten centuries of French ecclesiastical architecture, from its beginnings as a small Christian church during Charlemagne's reign in the 7th century to a plethora of additions and embellishments ranging from a 14th-century nave to 17th-century cloisters and 18th-century wooden choir stalls. Underground passages allow visitors to discover the abbey's earliest foundations, and outside there is a beautiful cloister garden, restored in 2007.
Ruelle du Monestier. Tel: (0468) 78 09 44. Email: abbayecaunesminervois@ orange.fr. Open: Feb, Mar, Nov & Dec daily 10am–noon & 2–5pm; Apr–Jun, Sept & Oct daily 10am–noon & 2–6pm; Jul & Aug daily 10am–7pm.

Minerve
Perched dramatically atop the steep grey limestone cliffs of a canyon carved by the Cesse river, Minerve is a perfect natural defensible position, and so it became a Cathar stronghold. Besieged by the forces of Simon de Montfort in 1210 at the beginning of the Albigensian Crusade, it held out for five months despite being bombarded by a massive boulder-hurling ballista which was aptly nicknamed the 'Malvoisine' ('Bad Neighbour'). When it finally fell, its surviving defenders reputedly threw themselves into the

The dramatic tower at Minerve

bonfire that had been built to burn them, in a last act of defiance.

Montagne Noire
This range of hills rises steeply from the Aude valley just north of Carcassonne. Thickly forested with Spanish chestnut, it is rich in wildlife and has some great waymarked walking trails. There are only a few small villages in the Montagne Noire, and its streams and woods are favoured by hunters and fishermen. A few kilometres north of

(*Cont. on p112*)

Wines and vineyards of Languedoc

By rights, Languedoc-Roussillon's wines and vineyards should be better known and more widely appreciated. This is, after all, one of the oldest winemaking areas in the world, with almost 3,000sq km (1,160sq miles) of land under vines, making it the world's largest grape-growing region (three times the size of the much more famous Bordeaux). It's estimated that around one third of the wine drunk in France, and around 10 per cent of the wine drunk around the world, is produced here. With its widely differing varieties of soil and microclimates, the region's vineyards produce an array of distinctive red, white and rosé wines, sparkling *crémant* (a term which refers to sparkling wines not made in the Champagne region) and luscious *vin doux* (dessert wines).

A stack of wine barrels

Languedoc is still battling to throw off its long-standing reputation as a purveyor of floods of cheap, generic *vin de table* (table wine), but it has a portfolio of quite outstanding wines to be proud of. Local winemakers fiercely defend their AOC (Appellation d'Origine Contrôlée, meaning 'controlled designation of origin') and Vin de Pays status, and point out that on occasion their product has been bought in bulk, relabelled and passed off as *Grand Cru* Bordeaux by unscrupulous merchants. Vin de Pays d'Oc (red, white and rosé) has become one of Europe's favourite labels (at least in terms of bottles sold), appearing on supermarket shelves and restaurant wine lists all over the world.

The key grape varieties grown in the region include the ubiquitous Syrah, Grenache, Cabernet-Sauvignon and Merlot, which form the mainstay of the cheaper *vins de pays* and *vins de table*. Carignan vines cover vast acreages and go into heavy-duty red wines such as Fitou, Languedoc's first red wine AOC region, while Cinsault grapes give a somewhat less chewy texture to lighter reds.

After Fitou, Languedoc-Roussillon's best-known *appellations* include

Wine shops, like this one in Carcassonne, are kept well stocked

Minervois and Corbières, both of which produce some tasty products. The Minervois occupies a huge sweep of sunny, south-facing vineyards on the arid hillsides north and south of Carcassonne and produces mostly reds, which range from cheap, downmarket picnic wines to some really high-quality names from La Livinière area, below Minerve. To the south, the Corbières vineyards, with their long, hot summers and harsh limestone soils, produce red wines rich in character and ideal as an accompaniment to *cassoulet*, game and steak.

The region as a whole produces fewer white wines, but the Costières de Nîmes region produces – in addition to its Rhône-like reds – some lovely, perfumed whites that are perfect as an apéritif or with seafood. Better known are the *méthode ancestrale* sparkling white wines of Limoux, made mainly from Chardonnay grapes and drunk in quantity all over the region as an affordable – and delightfully quaffable – alternative to Champagne. From the Roussillon slopes of Banyuls, Maury and Rivesaltes come some of France's best-loved dessert wines. Created mainly from Grenache Noir, these fortified wines are high in alcohol, rich in fruit and flavour, and go perfectly with sweet desserts and cheeses to round off a meal. They age and keep well, and are usually sold in smaller half-litre bottles, so they are also ideal purchases to take home as a delicious souvenir.

Lastours, it's worth stopping in Ilhes-Cabardès to visit its *Syndicat d'Initiative* (impossible to miss on the main road through the tiny village), which functions as a tourist office for most of the region, offering a rack full of free maps and information leaflets. The prettier and even tinier village of Roquefère has one excellent restaurant and a small shop which sells wine, cold drinks and local specialities.

The hills of the Montagne Noire rise to their highest point at the Pic de Nore (*see p116*), roughly midway between Carcassonne and Mazamet. Below the

Minerve's impressive battlements

peak, the Lac de Pradelles offers swimming, a campsite and a small café-restaurant in summer.
24km (15 miles) north of Carcassonne/ 23km (14 miles) south of Mazamet.

Gouffre Géant de Cabrespine (Giant Underground Cave of Cabrespine)
This enormous cave complex has some of the most breathtaking crystal formations in the world, which glitter beneath a state-of-the-art computer-controlled lighting system. Its main chamber is 250m (820ft) high – tall enough to accommodate the Eiffel Tower, according to the guides.
Cabrespine. Tel: (0468) 26 14 22. www.grottes-de-france.com. Open: Feb, Mar & Nov–mid-Dec daily 2–5.30pm; Apr–Jun, Sept & Oct daily 10.30am– 5.30pm; Jul & Aug daily 10.15am– 6pm. Closed: mid-Dec–end Jan. Admission charge.

Grotte de Limousis (Limousis Cave)
The Grotte de Limousis is the largest visitor-accessible cave in France, with a 1km (²/₃-mile) underground walkway that connects five vast caverns and two subterranean lakes, lined with spectacular rock and crystal formations. There is evidence that the cavern was used by prehistoric people. Early aristocratic visitors carved their names into the stalactites, local villagers held dances in the cave known as the *salle du bal* (ballroom), and the winemakers of Limousis found that

the stable 14°C (57°F) temperature within the grotto was perfect for ageing their wines.
Cabrespine. Tel: (0468) 26 14 20. www.grottes-de-france.com. Open: Mar & Oct daily 2.30–5.30pm; Apr–Jun & Sept daily 10.30am–5.30pm; Jul & Aug daily 10.15am–6pm. Closed: Dec–Feb. Admission charge.

Les Lamas de la Montagne Noire (Montagne Noire Llamas)

A herd of tame Andean llamas flourishes happily amid the woods, hills and pastures of the Montagne Noire. Guided visits explain the animals' long relationship with humanity and show how they are raised and trained, and families and groups (minimum four people) can go on a short or longer half-day llama trek on the walking trails of the Montagne Noire, learning along the way how to lead a llama and discovering the plants and other animals of the region.
Route de Pradelles (D89), Castans. Tel: (0468) 26 60 11. www.multimania. com/lamabalade. Open: French school holidays daily 9am–sunset; rest of the year daily 2pm–sunset. Admission charge (free for children under 12 accompanied by adults).

A Romanesque church peeks out from the trees in the Montagne Noire

Carcassonne and the Aude valley

Haut-Languedoc

North of the watershed of the Montagne Noire, Haut-Languedoc is a vast area that combines wide areas of forested hills, fertile farmland, thinly inhabited highlands, deep valleys and some of Languedoc's prettiest hill villages. Much of the region lies within the borders of the Parc Naturel Régional du Haut-Languedoc, a region of lakes, deep gorges, high hills and hidden valleys, which abounds in wildlife and offers some of the best hiking in Languedoc-Roussillon.

This is a region which is often overlooked by visitors who have been seduced by the charms of the Mediterranean beaches or drawn to the high-profile attractions of Languedoc-Roussillon's better-known cities and heritage attractions. But for those who are prepared to travel a little bit off the beaten track, it offers rich rewards. Remote though this part of the world may seem at a first glance at the map, most of Haut-Languedoc is easily accessible by bus or train (though using a hired car does make it even easier). Tucked away in its wooded valleys are some of the most picturesque villages in France. In summer, the beaches on the shores of the region's artificial lakes are less crowded than the sands of the Mediterranean shore, and provide fun for all the family, whether you're in the mood for shallow warm waters where toddlers can splash about, or exciting watersports for teens and adults. Haut-Languedoc has its own portfolio of hidden histories, too, but this part of Languedoc-Roussillon is above all a destination for open-air activities and adventures.

Mazamet

Mazamet is a thriving market town, and although it's well off the beaten tourist track it is a popular base for an array of open-air activities ranging from canyoning and canoeing to fishing, riding and walking on the long-distance trails that bypass the town. There's a lively and colourful Saturday morning market, and a number of shops sell the sheepskins and leatherwear for which

The bustling market in Mazamet

Mazamet is well known. The town made its fortune from the wool and felt-making industries, and a number of warehouse stores just north of town, close to the picturesque fortress-village of Hautpoul, sell quality sheepskins at outlet prices.

Office de Tourisme, 3 rue des Casernes. Tel: (0563) 61 27 07.
www.tourisme-mazamet.com

Maison du Bois et du Jouet (House of Wood and Toys)

Aimed mainly at children, this museum displays more than 1,200 wooden playthings from all over the world. It also has an arboretum, a picnic area, and access to 19km (12 miles) of waymarked woodland walking trails.

Moulin d'Oule, 3km (2 miles) south of Mazamet. Tel: (0563) 61 42 70.
www.hautpoul.org. Open: Jan–Jun & Sept–Dec Wed, Sat & Sun 2–6pm; Jul & Aug daily 2–7pm. Free admission.

Maison des Mémoires de Mazamet (Mazamet House of Memories)

Sharing a gracious historic mansion with the tourist office, the Maison des Mémoires combines two rooms which re-create the style of a wealthy 19th-century family, with an exhibition revealing the truth behind many of the

See pp124–7 for walk route

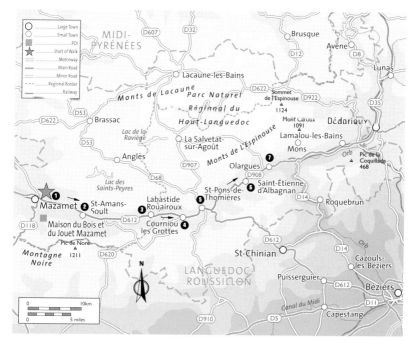

View of the Pic de Nore from across the Lac de Pradelles

myths surrounding the Cathars of the region and their faith.

Maison Fuzier, 3 rue des Casernes. Tel: (0563) 61 56 56. www.maison-memoires.com. Open: Feb, Mar, Nov & Dec Wed–Sat 2.30–5.30pm; Apr, May, Sept & Oct Wed–Sun 2.30–5.30pm; Jun–Aug Mon–Fri 10am–noon & 2.30–6pm, Sat–Sun 3–6pm. Closed: Jan. Admission charge.

La Moutonnerie

The museum traces the history of Mazamet's wool and sheepskin industry from its heyday in the 19th century to its decline in recent years. 'Moutonnerie' is a familiar term that can only really be translated as 'sheeplike simplicity or silliness' – a quirkily apt name for this interesting museum.

24 rue de la Ferronnerie. Tel: (0563) 61 02 43. www.castres-mazamet.fr. Open: Sept–Jun Mon–Fri 3.30–5.30pm; Jul & Aug

Mon–Fri 10am–noon & 3–6.30pm. Admission charge.

Pic de Nore

At 1,211m (3,973ft) the Pic de Nore is just 133m (436ft) lower than Ben Nevis. It is the highest point of the Montagne Noire and the entire Haut-Languedoc, and is easily visible as far away as Carcassonne – partly because it is crowned by a tall, red-and-white-striped telecommunications tower. It may be white with snow or frost as late into the year as April, when the valleys below are already in spring bloom, and from its summit on a clear day there are views all the way to the plains of the Aude and the peaks of Pyrénées to the south and across the fertile lowlands, and to the north to the rugged terrain of Haut-Languedoc's Parc Naturel Régional. The peak lies right on the park's southern boundary. Its northern slopes are cloaked in thick woods of chestnut, oak and conifers (the Forêt de Nore) and are almost uninhabited except for a few tiny hamlets. The long-distance GR36 walking trail traverses the peak (*www.gr-infos.com*).

17km (10½ miles) southeast of Mazamet on the D87.

Parc Naturel Régional du Haut-Languedoc (Haut-Languedoc Regional Natural Park)

Opened in 1973 and expanded in 1999, the regional park now embraces 2,600sq km (1,000sq miles) of streams, deep canyons, meadows, pastures, fields and forests. It is not a pure wilderness area: there are more than 90 towns, villages and hamlets within its boundaries, including Mazamet, the largest town in the area. Above all, it is easily accessible, with the D612/D908 main road from Mazamet to Clermont-l'Hérault running all the way along its southern edge.

Straddling the two *départements* of Tarn in the west and Hérault in the east, the park comprises a range of diverse areas including the northern slopes of the Montagne Noire and the Sidobre area in the west, the Monts de Lacaune along the northern edge of the park and the Vignes et Vallées area, bordering the vineyards of the upper Hérault valley. The eastern part of the park is dominated by two high peaks, the 1,124m (3,688ft) Sommet de l'Espinouse and the 1,091m (3,579ft) Mont Caroux. Around 20 walking trails traverse the length and breadth of

the park, and detailed guides to recommended routes, complete with reliable maps, are sold (currently for the token price of €1) at the park headquarters and at the tourist offices in the villages of Saint-Pons-de-Thomières and Olargues. The Voie Verte 'Passa Païs' follows the line of the railway which ran between Mazamet and Bédarieux until 1986. It is some 80km (50 miles) long, but avoids steep ascents and descents, so it is fairly easy-going and is popular with walkers, cyclists and horse riders.

In the centre of the Parc Naturel Régional, the Plateau des Lacs is a region of man-made lakes that offer canoeing, swimming and fishing in

(*Cont. on p120*)

The church at Saint-Pons-de-Thomières

Wildlife of Haut-Languedoc

With its astonishing range of microclimates and environments, from dry maquis and barren crests to thick deciduous and conifer forests, lakes and rivers, the Parc Naturel Régional du Haut-Languedoc is home to an equally wide assortment of plant and animal species – 2,500 in all, not counting insects and other inverterbrates. Large mammals include the ubiquitous *sanglier* (wild boar) and *chevreuil* (roe deer), and the much rarer *mouflon* (wild mountain sheep) and *genette* (European genet), as well as foxes, badgers and red squirrels. The park is also home to some spectacular birds and reptiles. Numerous raptor species frequent the park's skies, including peregrine falcons, booted eagles and royal eagles in the Espinouse region, and even the very rare Bonelli's eagle.

Two species of venomous snake may be seen, though neither the Montpellier snake (one of the largest European serpents) nor the common adder are aggressive, and their bite is rarely lethal. Other reptiles include the vividly hued green lizard and the eyed lizard, and equally colourful amphibians such as the green-and-black patterned marbled newt and the yellow-and-black spotted salamander.

For many visitors, especially children, the insect life of Languedoc can be fascinating. As well as hundreds of butterflies, including rarities such as the anomalous blue – which is in fact a sooty black colour – and beauties such as the purple emperor, there are some magnificent night-flying moths such as the great peacock or emperor moth, and a number of spectacular hawk moths, including the death's-head hawk moth with its skull-like markings. Bug-eyed preying mantises stalk smaller insects in grassy fields, where vivid green crickets also lurk, and on rocky paths perfectly camouflaged grasshoppers often leap up in showers, flashing bright turquoise and scarlet underwings. Among the most striking insect species are the

A friendly spotted salamander

If you're lucky enough, you may spot a purple emperor butterfly

ferocious-looking stag beetle and the great Capricorn, both of which lay their eggs in rotten wood in order to nourish their grubs.

The range of wildlife to be seen changes with the seasons, with many smaller creatures spending the winter in hibernation, while many bird species spend only summer or winter in the park. Swallows, house martins, sand martins and swifts arrive in spring, along with cuckoos, whose distinctive call is heard in the valleys from early April. The drumming sound of woodpeckers working at dead timber is another spring feature, while the shrill and discordant call of the black redstart, with its habit of nesting in dilapidated buildings, earns it the ironic French nickname *rossignol des murailles* ('nightingale of the ruins').

There is plenty of wildlife beyond the boundaries of the Haut-

Languedoc regional park too, especially in the thick woods of the Montagne Noire, which are also a happy hunting ground for local *chasseurs* (hunters) in hot pursuit of wild boar in late summer, autumn and winter. While some visitors may find the French fondness for hunting repugnant, local people point out that there are now more boar than ever – the *sanglier* population is estimated at around 40,000 for the whole region, even though hunters account for more than 16,000 every year. Unfortunately, shooting accidents are not uncommon, and those planning to venture off the beaten track and into the woods during the shooting season should use caution and wear conspicuous clothing ('blaze orange' is recommended) to avoid being mistaken for a wandering boar.

summer, and the small village of La Salvetat-sur-Agoût, midway along the magnificent walking trails which run east–west across the park, has become a miniature outdoor activity resort by virtue of its location at the east end of the fjord-like Lac de la Raviège. With a good choice of places to stay (ranging from campsites to *gîtes* and holiday apartments) and several companies renting boats, bikes and canoes, this is the best base for a longer stay in the park.

Maison du Parc (Park Headquarters), 1 place Foirail, Saint-Pons-de-Thomières. Tel: (0467) 97 38 22. www.parc-haut-languedoc.fr. Open: Mon–Fri 8am–noon & 1.30–6pm.

The delightful village of Olargues

Saint-Pons-de-Thomières

Saint-Pons-de-Thomières is the main gateway to the Parc Naturel Régional du Haut-Languedoc, but it is also a very pretty (and very sunny) village with a small but select collection of attractions that make it well worth a visit in its own right. Those heading on into the park should first visit the Maison du Parc (*see above*), which has a great assortment of free information, maps and guides. Opposite the park headquarters is the vast 12th-century cathedral, which dominates the old town.

Office de Tourisme, Place Foirail. Tel: (0467) 97 06 65. www.saint-pons-tourisme.com. Open: Tue–Fri 9am–noon & 2–6pm, Sat 9–noon & 2–5pm. Closed: Sun.

Musée Français de la Spéléologie (Speleology Museum of France) and Grotte de la Devèze (Devèze Cave)

Haut-Languedoc, like much of Languedoc-Roussillon, is riddled with caverns and grottoes. The Grotte de la Devèze is an impressive subterranean hall, festooned with rock formations that resemble frozen waterfalls. The cave's own museum is dedicated to the history of underground exploration, with an astonishing collection of finds, including skulls and skeletons of long-extinct prehistoric cave-dwelling creatures.

Avenue d'Occitanie, Courniou-les-Grottes, 5km (3 miles) west of Saint-Pons-de-Thomières on the D612, signposted from the village centre. Tel: (0467) 97 03 85.

www.saint-pons-tourisme.com.
Open: hours vary, so call or enquire at
tourist office.

Musée de Préhistoire Régionale
(**Regional Prehistory Museum**)
Housed partly in a medieval building
opposite the cathedral and partly in a
modern purpose-built wing, this
bright, well-laid-out museum traces the
history of human habitation in the
mountains of Haut-Languedoc and the
surrounding regions back over more
than 5,000 years, with galleries of
Neolithic tools, weapons and skulls,
menhirs, and interactive displays.
8 Grand'rue. Tel: (0467) 97 22 61.
www.saint-pons-tourisme.com.
Open: Apr–mid-Jun & mid-Sept–end
Oct Tue–Sun 3–6pm; mid-Jun–mid-Sept
Tue–Sun 10am–noon & 3–6pm.
Closed: Mon & Nov–end Mar.
Admission charge.

Olargues
Olargues is one of the prettiest of the
old villages dotted along the southern
fringe of the park, with a landmark
clock tower poised above a clutter of tall
old houses where a 13th-century stone
bridge, the Pont du Diable ('Devil's
Bridge') crosses the river. It is a handy
gateway to the hill country of the Monts
de l'Espinouse and the deep canyons of
the Gorges d'Héric, and although it has
few outstanding sights in its own right,
it is a very pleasant stop when travelling
along the D612 route, and makes for a
good overnight break.

42km (26 miles) east of Mazamet on the
D612. Office de Tourisme, Avenue de la
Gare. Tel: (0467) 97 71 26.
www.olargues.org. Open: Jun & Sept
Tue–Sun 3–6pm; Oct–May Tue–Sat
10am–noon & 2–6pm; Jul & Aug daily
9.30am–1pm & 4–7pm.

Musée d'Arts et Traditions Populaires
(**Museum of Folk Arts and Traditions**)
This excellent little museum, set up by
the villagers themselves to keep the
memory of the village's recent past
alive, is packed with fascinating
memorabilia, including traditional
farm tools and household utensils
that were still in use until the
mid-20th century, old family photos,
and fossils and relics of the first
Neolithic people who settled in the
Haut-Languedoc region between
2000 and 1500 BC.
Escaliers de la Commanderie.
www.olargues.org. Open: mid-Jun–end
Sept Tue–Sun 3–6pm. Free admission.

Roquebrun
Midway down the valley of the Orb
and surrounded by the vineyards of the
Saint-Chinian AOC, Roquebrun is a
seductively attractive spot, with tiers of
colourfully painted houses rising above
a wide, shallow bend in the river, which
at this point creates a broad pebbly
beach where you can sunbathe and
where children can splash and paddle
(though it's too shallow for swimming).
Upstream from the arched stone bridge
which crosses the river at this point, the

Roquebrun offers canoeing, wine-tasting and a relaxing environment

river is deeper, wider and faster-flowing, making Roquebrun a magnet for canoeists, who start their journey at Moulins (7km/4½ miles east of Olargues) then float down the serpentine, jade-green Orb for some 24km (15 miles) to Roquebrun. Several companies offer canoe rental for experienced canoeists, and guided trips for novices. Above the town stands a gaunt tower, which is all that remains of the 10th–11th-century castle built by the Trencavel dynasty of Carcassonne. Roquebrun is the capital of its own Appellation d'Origine Contrôlée wine area, AOC Saint-Chinian-Roquebrun, and there are eight different wine-tasting *caves* (cellars) and domains in and around the village.

23km (14 miles) south of Mons on the D14. Office de Tourisme, 4 avenue des Orangers. Tel: (0467) 23 02 21. Email: office-tourisme-roquebrun@wanadoo.fr

Cave de Roquebrun
Handily located just a short distance from the centre of the village, this wine boutique offers tastings of the Saint-Chinian AOC red, white and rosé wines as well as its unique Roche Brune XO *eau de vie*.

Avenue des Orangers. Tel: (0467) 89 64 35. www.cave-roquebrun.fr. Open: May, Jun, Sept & Oct daily 9.30am–1pm & 2.30–7pm; Jul & Aug daily 9am–1pm & 3–7.30pm; Nov–Apr Mon–Sat 9.30am–12.30pm & 2–6pm, Sun 10.30am–12.30pm & 2–6pm. Free admission.

Jardin Méditerranéen (Mediterranean Garden)
Roquebrun's clement microclimate not only allows the vineyards of

Saint-Chinian to flourish but also nurtures an impressive array of Mediterranean and subtropical plants. The Jardin Méditerranéen is a remarkable collection of plants from all over the Mediterranean, Africa, Asia, Australia and the Americas.

Rue de la Tour. Tel: (0467) 89 55 29. www.jardin-mediterraneen.fr. Open: mid-Feb–Jun & Sept–mid-Nov Sun–Fri 9am–noon & 12.30–5.30pm, Sat 12.30–5.30pm; Jul & Aug daily 9am–7pm. Closed: mid-Nov–mid-Feb. Admission charge.

Lamalou-les-Bains

Lamalou-les-Bains is an orderly spa town which flourished in the 19th century – as evidenced by the plethora of belle-époque buildings scattered around its gracious, peaceful town centre, including a grand theatre, a casino and two ornate bandstands which still provide a venue for occasional musical performances in summer. Two colossal Egyptian-style reliefs of water goddesses are carved into the stonework of the rail bridge that crosses the river at this point. The supposed healing powers of the town's thermal springs still attract numbers of elderly French people seeking relief from arthritis, rheumatism and other aches and pains, but for healthier visitors it is also a useful starting point for a hike into the Parc Naturel Régional du Haut-Languedoc.

57km (35 miles) east of Mazamet on the D908. Office de Tourisme, 1 avenue Capus. Tel: (0467) 95 70 91. www.ot-lamaloulesbains.fr

Lacaune-les-Bains

Like Lamalou-les-Bains, Lacaune-les-Bains has been a spa town for centuries. Today, though, it is of more interest to visitors as a jumping-off point for exploring the northern reaches of the Parc Naturel Régional du Haut-Languedoc and the Monts de Lacaune. The milk of the flocks of sheep that graze on the high pastures around Lacaune goes to make Roquefort, probably France's most famous blue cheese, and the region is also renowned for its *charcuterie* (cooked pork meats).

41km (25 miles) north of Saint-Pons-de-Thomières on the D907, via La Salvetat-sur-Agoût. Office de Tourisme, Place Général de Gaulle. Tel: (0563) 37 04 98. www.lacaune.com

Maison de la Charcuterie (House of Pork)

The delicious ham from the free-range, acorn-fed pigs which are reared in the woodlands around Lacaune is a gourmet item. It can be sampled at the Maison de la Charcuterie, where a six-room exhibition explains every aspect of pig-rearing and charcuterie-making from the Middle Ages to the present day.

3 rue Biarnes. Tel: (0563) 37 46 31. www.lacaune.com. Open: mid-Jun–mid-Sept 10am–noon & 2.30–6pm. Admission charge.

Walk: Voie Verte 'Passa Païs'

This easy-going itinerary follows the line of the old railway track which skirts the southern perimeter of the Parc Naturel Régional du Haut-Languedoc, passing through some of the region's prettiest villages and with plenty of places to stay and eat along the way. It starts at 256m (840ft) above sea level, rising to 400m (1,310ft) at its highest point. The route can be travelled on foot or by bike.

It is at its best in summer, but rain is possible at any time and a waterproof jacket is essential. The path is prominently signposted all the way, and passes through a number of railway tunnels which are automatically illuminated as you walk through them.

The distance covered is 50km (31 miles) and should take three days, with stops included. See map on p115.

Start at Mazamet.

1 Mazamet

Mazamet (*see pp114–16*) is an attractive small town with a bustling Saturday morning market that spills out into the streets around its main square. It is the commercial hub of the western part of Haut-Languedoc, and lies within the boundaries of the Parc Naturel. Before setting out, visit the local tourist office and the Maison des Mémoires, which are housed in the same building on Rue des Casernes (*see pp115–16*).

Begin the walk by following the Voie Verte out of town and continue for 1km (²⁄₃ mile) to Bout-du-Pont-de-l'Arn. Passing through this suburb, carry on eastward for 8km (5 miles) to Saint-Amans-Soult, passing through the lush pastures and cornfields of the Thore valley, with the slopes of the Montagne Noire and the Pic de Nore to the south.

2 Saint-Amans-Soult

The main attraction in this otherwise unassuming spot is the Château de Soult-Berg, the lavish home of Maréchal Nicolas Soult, born in Saint-Amans (1769–1851). During his career as one of Napoleon's favoured marshals, Soult cherished dreams of becoming King of Spain, but his defeats at the hands of the Duke of Wellington put paid to those hopes. Nevertheless, the château is clearly the home of a man with expensive tastes, and there are guided tours of its opulent salons. Tour times and days change, so check at the tourist office

The headquarters of the Parc National Régional du Haut-Languedoc in Saint-Pons-de-Thomières

The bridge and cherry orchards at Saint-Étienne-d'Albagnan

in Mazamet if you plan to make this a part of your itinerary.

Continue east along the Voie Verte for 9km (5½ miles) through fields and woodland to the small village of Lacabarède, then for a further 5km (3 miles) to Labastide Rouairoux. The trail rises gently to 400m (1,310ft) above sea level.

3 Labastide Rouairoux

The Voie Verte takes you into the heart of this former weaving village, which once provided fine woollen cloth for the *couturiers* of Paris. Today, Labastide Rouairoux is the nexus of a web of walking routes leading into the Parc Naturel Régional du Haut-Languedoc. *Leaving Labastide Rouairoux, walk through the woods to the entrance of a 766m (2,513ft) former railway tunnel which burrows under the pass of the*

Col de la Fenille (note that this tunnel is illuminated only until 7pm).

About 7km (4½ miles) after leaving the tunnel, enter the tiny village of Courniou-les-Grottes on a path which slopes gently downhill through woods.

4 Courniou-les-Grottes

As the path enters the village, pause to visit the Musée Français de la Spéléologie (*see pp120–21*), where you can marvel at the boldness of early cave-explorers who plunged deep underground using rather primitive equipment. Then visit the remarkable Grotte de la Devèze (*see pp120–21*), which was discovered in 1886 during the building of the railway line. *Carry on for 6km (4 miles) as the route winds towards Saint-Pons-de-Thomières, passing through three short tunnels.*

Walk: Voie Verte 'Passa País'

5 Saint-Pons-de-Thomières

Saint-Pons-de-Thomières (*see p120*) is the main gateway to the Parc National Régional du Haut-Languedoc and the seat of the park headquarters. A river flows through the middle of this charming village, where a 12th-century cathedral dominates the old town. It is worth taking the time here to visit the park headquarters and the next-door Musée de Préhistoire Régionale.

Carry on downhill along the north bank of the Jaur valley for 8km (5 miles), bypassing the small village of Riols (on the opposite bank) and passing through the lovely little village of Prémian (where parts of the Voie Verte may be used by vehicles). 3km (just under 2 miles) east of Prémian, you will arrive in Saint-Étienne-d'Albagnan.

6 Saint-Étienne-d'Albagnan

The narrow streets of this little hill village on the south bank of the Jaur are dotted with medieval churches, and cherry orchards cover the slopes on either side of the valley. Detour to your right if you wish to stroll through the village, then return to the Voie Verte.

Leaving Saint-Étienne-d'Albagnan, walk through the fourth tunnel along this route, then up a steep slope which bypasses yet another tunnel, taking you to the highest point of the walk, with great views of the wooded Jaur valley and its cherry orchards. Carry on for 8km (5 miles), trending downhill all the way, to Olargues.

7 Olargues

The 13th-century Pont du Diable ('Devil's Bridge'), arching across the river, and the ancient clock tower above it are the landmarks for the last stop on this walk. From here, energetic walkers can plunge onward to the rugged hills of the Monts de l'Espinouse or the deep canyons of the Gorges d'Héric, while others can return to Mazamet or travel on by bus to Béziers or Nîmes. If none of that appeals, just relax in Olargues for a while and enjoy one of the prettiest villages in France (*see p121*).

The grand theatre at Lamalou-les-Bains

The hunt for fungus

France has hundreds of kinds of edible (and delicious) wild fungus, but of them all the cep (*Boletus edulis*) and the truffle (*Tuber melanosporum*) are the most famous and sought-after. French villagers seek them eagerly, town and city dwellers make special fungus-gathering trips into the countryside, and the location of a particularly productive patch of woodland is often a jealously guarded secret. This is hardly surprising, considering that some fungus species fetch a handsome price in local markets.

The cep is also known in English as the 'penny bun' fungus, and it really does look very like a brown, shiny bun. With a mild, slightly nutty flavour, they can be eaten raw and thinly sliced in a salad, fried in oil or butter with parsley and garlic, grilled and served with fish, or preserved by drying and used to add flavour to soups and stews. As with all wild fungi, it is important to be absolutely sure that the harvested specimens are from an edible species, as some of the Boletus family – especially the Devil's bolete (*Boletus satanas*) can be poisonous. Fortunately, with its nasty smell and yellowish flesh that turns blue when cut, it is easy to tell the Devil's bolete from its tasty cousin. To be on the safe side, you can take your finds to one of the many pharmacies that offer a fungus identification service.

Many French fungus-gatherers hunt only for *cèpes* (ceps), which start to emerge in early autumn and grow most prolifically in the leaf-litter at the foot of chestnut trees. The woods of the Montagne Noire are a favourite spot for finding a good harvest. But chestnut woods also produce the easily identified rich yellow or orange *girolles* (chanterelles) and the black *trompettes de mort* ('trumpets of death'), both of which are also good eating, despite the foreboding name of the latter. Generally, the best time for fungus-gathering is late September, but a dry autumn may lead to a late or sparse crop. If you're staying in promising territory in the Languedoc hill country in fungus season, the best time of day to go gathering is in the morning after a day of light showers – heavy rain, however, can reduce a promising patch of ceps or *girolles* to unappetising slime. If you have time before you leave, or if you're travelling with your own car, any fungi that you don't eat right away can easily be dried and used later.

A basket of truffles – the 'black gold' of Languedoc

If ceps are valued, truffles – 'black gold' – are prized above all other fungi. In Languedoc, the area around Uzès, north of Nîmes, is legendary for its truffles (*see pp38–9*), and a busy truffle market is held in the town on the third Sunday of January each year, when truffles are held to be at their best and when hunters from all over the region bring their prize finds to sell to connoisseurs and restaurateurs from all over France. Truffles grow underground, among the roots of oak trees, and the truffle-hunters of Uzès use pigs as well as dogs to sniff them out. During the truffle festival, Place aux Herbes, the town's central square, is used for truffle-hunting demonstrations, when trained pigs search for fungi which have been specially buried around the square. Black truffles can grow to a size of 7cm (2³/₄ inches) across, and may weigh up to 100g (3¹/₂ ounces). Good specimens cost up to €1,000 per kilogram in local markets, so a 100g truffle is a rewarding find for any hunter. Prices can, however, vary widely from year to year, rising sharply in a bad harvest year, or dropping again when there is a glut of truffles on the market.

Getting away from it all

Languedoc-Roussillon's major towns and cities bustle with tourism almost all year round. In high season, Carcassonne's Cité Médiévale and other historic centres such as Nîmes are thronged with visitors, and in July and August even the long, spacious beaches of the Roussillon coast can seem crowded, while a cavalcade of walkers and cyclists take to the most popular mountain trails which criss-cross the most accessible regional park areas of Haut-Languedoc and the Pyrénées-Orientales.

This may sound worrying to those in search of tranquil solitude, but Languedoc-Roussillon covers a vast area of wide, open spaces and coasts, and even at the peak of the holiday season it is possible to get away from the crowds.

Les Saintes-Maries and the Parc Naturel Régional de Camargue (Camargue Regional Natural Park)

Technically, Les Saintes-Maries-de-la-Mer and the Camargue lie just beyond the eastern border of Languedoc-Roussillon, at the mouth of the Rhône delta. That should not deter anyone in search of perfect beachcombing coastline and scenery that is unlike anywhere else in France.

The small seaside resort of Les Saintes-Maries-de-la-Mer, 31km (19 miles), southeast of Aigues-Mortes on the D58/D570, makes a convenient base for exploring the Parc Naturel Régional de Camargue, an 84,800-hectare

Les Saintes-Maries-de-la-Mer is a pleasant seaside resort

(209,545-acre) expanse of shallow lagoons, salt marshes and rice fields which is bounded in the east by the Grand Rhône, the main channel of the river. A long sandy spit sweeps eastward from Les Saintes-Maries, and while the sand and pebble section nearest to the resort gets busy in summer, there are emptier stretches further east (a fact that has not escaped naturist sunbathers in search of an all-over tan).

There are plenty of places to stay and eat in Les Saintes-Maries, including a pleasant campsite right on the edge of the natural park, which is home to flocks of flamingos, egrets and other waterbirds. The black cattle and white horses that are symbolic of the Camargue are raised in numerous *manades* (ranches) around the Plaine de la Camargue, and many of them offer riding trips or horse-and-carriage tours. Several companies also offer boat trips on the lagoons.

Les Saintes-Maries is home to a historic fortified church, dedicated to Saint Mary Magdalene who, along with Saint Mary Martha, is said to have arrived here by sea in 18 AD to bring Christianity to the region. Inside the little whitewashed building there are charming, colourfully painted wooden statues of the sainted ladies. If you want to avoid crowds, don't visit in May, when the church is the focus of a gypsy pilgrimage which draws thousands of travelling folk from all over France, Spain and Portugal to the village.

The wild hills of the Cévennes

Saintes-Maries-de-la-Mer Office de Tourisme, 5 avenue van Gogh. Tel: (0490) 97 82 55. www.saintesmaries.com

The Cévennes

Stretching beyond Languedoc-Roussillon's northern borders, the Cévennes seems almost as wild and remote as it was when author Robert Louis Stevenson trekked across it in 1878, commemorating the trip in *Travels With a Donkey in the Cévennes*. The Parc National des Cévennes is an unspoilt, rugged region of forests and mountains, with many peaks rising to more than 1,300m (4,265ft). One of the park's big success stories since it was declared a national park in the 1960s has been the growth in numbers of some of the largest wild animals found in France: not just wild boar (which are common everywhere) but red deer, roe deer, *mouflon* (wild sheep) and *chamois*. There are some equally spectacular big birds, too, including three kinds of vulture, royal eagles and a number of

other raptors. Energetic walkers can follow in Robert Louis Stevenson's footsteps through the Cévennes on the Grande Randonnée 70 walking trail (*www.gr70-stevenson.com*).
Maison du Parc (Park Headquarters), 6 bis place de Palais, Florac.
Tel: (0466) 49 53 01.
www.cevennes-parcnational.fr

Sentier Cathare (Cathar Trail)

The Sentier Cathare is a spectacular and demanding walk between Foix in the Ariège region (69km/43 miles southwest of Carcassonne) and Port-la-Nouvelle on the Mediterranean coast (about 32km/20 miles south of Narbonne). On its way though the mountainous heartlands of Cathar country, it passes some of the most dramatic of the region's medieval castles, perched on the high crags of the Fenouillèdes and the Pays de Sault. For much of the route, the scenery is literally breathtaking: the least strenuous way to walk the route is to start at Foix and head east, with the terrain gradually becoming easier-going as you near the coast, and the promise of a dip in the Mediterranean at the end of the walk. From end to end, the Sentier Cathare is almost 240km (150 miles) in length, so those who plan to walk it need to be reasonably fit, and allow 10–12 days for the whole walk. However, there is adequate public transport (by train and bus) for much of the route and there are plenty of inns, *gîtes* and places to eat and drink along the way, so the trail need not be a severe endurance test.

Take a day out to see Andorra's unspoilt beauty

Andorra has well-equipped resorts in the heart of the mountains

Day trip to Andorra

High up in the Pyrénées, the tiny enclave of Andorra is a historical anomaly. It's also a great place for cheap shopping and affordable winter sports, and it's easily accessible from southern Languedoc and the coast.

It's worth visiting Andorra just to see one of the world's smallest countries: it is the sixth smallest in Europe, with a population of just 84,000 people (2010 estimate) and an area of only 468sq km (180sq miles). The Principality of Andorra, as it is technically known, was founded in 1278 and is co-governed by two 'princes', one of whom is the President of France, the other the Bishop of Urgell, in Spain. More than ten million people visit Andorra every year to buy low-priced cigarettes, spirits, perfumes and other goods that are sold tax-free, and to enjoy the winter sports offered by the principality's four main ski resorts. The ski season is generally from December to late March or even April, and the range of sports on offer also includes snowboarding, snow-shoeing, snowmobile safaris and even ice-diving in mountain lakes. There is plenty of purpose-built holiday accommodation in self-catering apartments and hotels, but in the busiest part of the winter-sports season, booking ahead is advisable, as most rooms are block-booked by package holiday companies. Andorra is not technically part of the euro zone, but it has no currency of its own, and so the euro is universally accepted.

The France–Andorra border crossing at Pas de la Casa is 135km (84 miles) north of Carcassonne. Andorra tourist office, Edifici Davi, Carrer del Doctor Vilanova 13. Tel: (00376) 82 02 14. www.andorra.ad

When to go

Languedoc-Roussillon can be visited year-round, but for most visitors it is at its most appealing from Easter to late October. Spring comes early, with average temperatures around 17°C (63°F) in April, and it's usually still warm and sunny well into late autumn, with average temperatures of 19°C (66°F) until October. In high summer, the average temperature is around 28°C (82°F), with peaks of 35°C (95°F) or even higher in July and August.

July and August are also the driest months of the year, but thunderstorms and spells of heavy rain are possible even in high summer, especially in the hilly north and west of the region. If sun and sand are your priorities, plan your trip for June, July and August, but make your travel and accommodation arrangements well in advance and don't expect to be alone – hundreds of thousands of French folk, as well as German, Dutch and Belgian visitors, throng to the Mediterranean beaches in high summer, and resorts, campsites

The Montagne Noire in winter can be bitterly cold

and roads will all be crowded. If you're planning to drive through France with your own car, avoid the days of *le départ* ('leaving', at the beginning of August) and *le retour* ('returning', at the end of the month), when the whole of France seems to be on the move and long traffic jams and delays are common on all routes to the south.

The region's festival season is in full swing by July, with dozens of events ranging from Carcassonne's spectacular Bastille Day pyrotechnics to local *fêtes* featuring music, dancing and communal dining in the village squares – the favourite time for which is mid-August.

For a walking or touring holiday, spring and autumn are the best choices, with mellow weather and fewer crowds at major sights and attractions such as Carcassonne's Cité Médiévale – and it's also easier to find affordable accommodation and cheaper rail and air fares outside the peak holiday season.

Bear in mind, too, that Languedoc-Roussillon is a patchwork of varied microclimates, with the hottest sunshine to be found on the coast and in the lowlands of the Aude. In summer, the high country of Haut-Languedoc and the even higher Pyrénées can be up to 5°C (9°F) cooler than the Mediterranean beaches, so if you plan to travel in summer and want to avoid extreme heat, head for the hills.

A pleasant short break can be enjoyed in towns and cities such as Carcassonne, Montpellier, Nîmes or Perpignan even in winter, but from November to February it's often too cold to enjoy a leisurely stroll or a drink at an outdoor café, with sub-zero daytime temperatures possible even in the lowlands, and plenty of snow in the mountains from December to March or even April, when the ski stations of the Pyrénées-Orientales and Andorra offer downhill and cross-country skiing.

Fares offered by no-frills airlines such as Ryanair and its rivals can vary widely even from day to day, but in general, air, train and ferry fare bargains are easier to find outside the main summer school holiday season. The Easter holiday period and the weeks before and after Christmas also tend to be expensive times to travel.

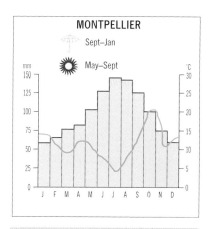

WEATHER CONVERSION CHART

25.4mm = 1 inch

°F = 1.8 × °C + 32

Getting around

Travelling between the larger towns and cities of Languedoc-Roussillon by public transport is fairly easy. Travelling village to village can be more of a challenge, however, and some smaller places in remoter areas have no public transport links at all. That said, if you really want to avoid the easiest option of renting a car (or bringing your own), a combination of rail, bus and the occasional taxi will take you to many of the places in this guide.

Tourist 'mini-trains' operate in summer within most major towns, making it easy to take in the sights without too much exertion, and are a boon for families with young children.

Trains

A main north–south railway line runs down the coast, connecting Nîmes with Montpellier, Béziers, Narbonne and Perpignan and smaller points in between. This route connects with an east–west main line at Narbonne, running through Carcassonne and Castelnaudary on its way to Toulouse. Another line loops westward from Perpignan through the Pyrénées via Prades, Ax-les-Thermes and Foix to Toulouse, while yet another local line loops southeast from Carcassonne through Limoux and Saint-Paul-de-Fenouillet to connect with the main coast line at Rivesaltes, just north of Perpignan.

Buses

Not all villages are served by bus routes, and where buses do operate to smaller communities their schedules are geared to taking villagers and schoolchildren into the nearest town early in the morning and bringing them back in late afternoon – not ideal timings for the sightseer or holidaymaker. Travelling between *départements* can also pose problems. Each *département* operates its separate bus network, with the result that it may be easy to travel some distance from a country village to the main town in its *département*, but impossible to go by bus to another town or village nearby that lies across the departmental boundary.

Taxis

Taxis are easy to find in all the main towns and cities, including Montpellier, Béziers, Nîmes, Narbonne, Perpignan and Carcassonne. They cannot be flagged down on the street, but are found at cab ranks at all the main stations, on or near the central square of each town, and at airports, where taxis meet every flight. Fares are metered and controlled by local authorities, and most drivers are willing to make longer trips to outlying villages as well as fares in town.

Self-driving

There are numerous car-rental companies in town centres and at all the region's airports. Bringing your own car to the region is easy enough, though it's a long drive from the Channel or Spanish ferry ports (*see 'Arriving and departing', pp154–5*). Make sure you have all the relevant paperwork (driving licence, vehicle registration documents and insurance certificate) at all times, as police spot checks are common. Random breath-testing for alcohol is also common: if you see oncoming drivers flashing their lights at you, they're probably warning that there's a police team lurking in wait for the

unwary. A crackdown on drink-driving in recent years has cut the death toll on France's roads by around half. Penalties are severe and the blood-alcohol limit is lower than in the UK, so it's best not to touch alcohol at all before driving. You should also carry a red warning triangle in case of breakdowns and a complete set of spare bulbs, and you'll need to adjust your headlight beams for driving on the right. Roads throughout Languedoc-Roussillon are generally excellent, but you will encounter narrow, winding hill roads in the Pyrénées, Haut-Languedoc and Lozère. Finding your way through the narrow, medieval streets and one-way systems of towns like Nimes or Carcassonne can be infuriatingly difficult: it's usually easier to use a car park on the outskirts of the historic centres and explore on foot.

Carcassonne's train station is busy and well connected

Accommodation

Languedoc-Roussillon offers every imaginable kind of place to stay, whether you're after grand and exclusive château-hotels, village inns, huge seaside holiday camps with supervised beaches, pools and lots of family activities, smaller campsites in the countryside, self-catering farmhouses, plush modern villas, budget pensions or modern city hotels. Accommodation standards are generally high, and can be surprisingly affordable.

Hotels

Hotels in France are officially graded in five categories, from 1-star to 4-star luxe, and are regularly inspected. However, the grading system is based on facilities in public areas (such as swimming pools, lifts, bars and restaurants) and in rooms (such as TV, en-suite shower and WC, minibar and direct-dial telephone), and on the size of the rooms, not on service standards. A 1-star *pension* is unlikely to have a bar, a restaurant or a lift, rooms will be small and may not have an en-suite shower or WC, while 4-star luxe hotels offer spacious rooms with all the trimmings, a choice of bars and restaurants, and usually have a spa, pool and gym. There are only a handful of 4-star luxe and 4-star properties in Languedoc-Roussillon, but these – like all France's best hotels – offer world-class service standards and facilities, including fine dining. Many smaller hotels belong to the **Logis de France** consortium, which independently grades its members from one to three

cheminées. Most of these are family-run and can be found throughout the region, and generally offer excellent value for money (*Central reservation service; tel: (0145) 84 83 84; www.logis-de-france.fr*).

In Languedoc-Roussillon's cities and larger towns – such as Carcassonne, Montpellier, Nîmes and Perpignan – places to stay range from stylish and luxurious boutique hotels within converted historic buildings to very basic 1-star *pensions*. Modern **4-star hotels** under the banners of major chains can be found in the region's biggest cities, and while these are aimed mainly at business travellers, they can sometimes offer excellent bargains at weekends and in summer, when business traffic is slow. Hotel chains such as Ibis and Mercure also offer **3-star accommodation** at strategic locations in city centres and airports. These can be good value for a short stay and usually offer a range of specially priced two- or three-night packages in low season and at weekends.

There are small **1- and 2-star pensions** – usually with no more than 20 rooms – in all the region's towns. These offer the most basic level of accommodation, with small bedrooms, usually without en-suite WC and shower. The oldest, cheapest and shabbiest of these are usually clustered near the train station, and are best avoided.

Modern **'no-frills' hotels** operated by a number of chains such as Formule 1, Campanile, Kyriade and Etap are handily located at main *autoroute* junctions, next to the region's airports, and on the outskirts of cities and larger towns. These offer very simple, clean and modern rooms, usually with a double bed and a bunk above, and are ideal for those arriving on a late-night flight, planning an early departure, or looking for a convenient one-night stop just off the *autoroute*. Bookable online, the cheapest and least-frilly versions are unstaffed at night and guests access the hotel and their rooms using a one-time PIN code. Even these, however, offer a simple self-service breakfast for a nominal price. Other city options include the comfortable, modern apartments of the Citadines chain, which have double bedrooms and a fully equipped sitting-room-kitchen with sofa bed.

Chambres d'hôtes

In smaller villages and in the countryside you will find plenty of

Le Terminus Hotel in Carcassonne

chambres d'hôtes, the French version of bed and breakfast, offering cosy rooms (not all with en-suite WC and shower) in family homes. All of these serve breakfast and many also provide dinner on request.

Holiday parks

Purpose-built holiday parks accommodate thousands of independent campers, motorhomes and caravans along large stretches of the Mediterranean coast between Cap d'Agde and Argelès-sur-Mer throughout the summer season. Most of these also offer family accommodation in 'mobile homes', the most luxurious of which sleep four to six people and have their own WC, shower and kitchenette. All offer facilities including supervised pools for younger children, large lagoon pools, stretches of supervised beach, watersports, mini-markets, bars, restaurants and self-service laundries. Most accommodation in these resorts is block-booked at least a year in advance, so for a holiday here your best bet is probably to book through one of the big holiday companies. Several 'textile-free' resorts around Cap d'Agde offer similar facilities for those who prefer not to wear clothes on or off the beach, even when shopping and socialising.

Chambres d'hôtes can be cosy and good value

CRUISING THE CANAL

One of the finest ways to see the Languedoc-Roussillon region is aboard a canal cruiser on the Canal du Midi. A wide range of boats is available, including modern purpose-built vessels – which sleep six to eight people and have galley kitchens and on-board showers and WC – traditional barges and full-service 'floating hotels' with luxurious cabins.

Campsites

There are also many smaller family campsites on the outskirts of the region's larger towns and in the hills of Haut-Languedoc and the Pyrénées-Orientales. These offer space for tents and motorhomes and most also have wooden chalets or mobile homes for rent. In the wilder parts of the region, a few quirky sites offer accommodation in tipis, treehouses or Mongolian-style yurts. The best are on lakeside sites, and many offer activities such as canoeing and kayaking. Most holiday parks and campsites are open only from mid-May to late September.

Youth hostels

There are a number of youth hostels offering dormitory bunks and family rooms around the region, mainly located in areas such as the Pyrénées-Orientales and Haut-Languedoc, along walking trails, and in natural parks. Many of these close during the winter, and booking is always advisable. Reservations can be made directly by phone or online, or through the **Fédération Unie des Auberges de Jeunesse** (FUAJ,

The Gîtes de France logo is a sign of family-friendly accommodation

French Youth Hostels Association, *www.fuaj.org*).

Gîtes

For families or groups of friends, renting a self-catering *gîte* in the countryside is a super option. These independently owned houses sleep up to 12 people and have fully equipped farmhouse kitchens and utility rooms with washer-dryers. The best even have swimming pools, games rooms and bicycles for guests. In cheaper *gîtes*, you must bring your own sheets and pillowcases, but most provide bed linen for a reasonable extra charge. Most *gîtes* close between October and Easter. The easiest way to book a *gîte* is through the ubiquitous **Gîtes de France** association, which has more than 3,250 member properties throughout Languedoc-Roussillon (*tel: (0468) 11 40 70 (Aude)/ (0467) 67 62 62 (Hérault)/(0468) 68 42 88 (Pyrénées-Orientales)/(0466) 27 94 94 (Gard)/(0466) 65 60 00 (Lozère). www.gites-de-france.com*).

Food and drink

Languedoc-Roussillon's patchwork of varied terrain and microclimates ensures a tremendous variety of local produce, and an equally exciting range of distinctive local dishes. From the lagoons of the Mediterranean coast come plump oysters and an array of other seafood. From the woods and pastures of the Montagne Noire come wild fungi and some of the best lamb in France. The Camargue is renowned for its black bull beef, while Castelnaudary is famed for its cassoulet.

Michelin-starred restaurants can be found across the region, but some of the best gourmet surprises are in small, family-run restaurants in quite out-of-the-way places, serving the best *cuisine du terroir* (regional cooking) from a menu that changes according to the seasons.

Specialities

One seasonal favourite is wild boar (*sanglier*), which is enthusiastically hunted in autumn and winter and appears on almost every table. Wild ceps, chanterelles, *trompettes de mort* and other fungi are eagerly sought in autumn, and the Uzège, north of Nîmes, is famed for its black truffles as well as for the olives that go to make the savoury paste called *tapenade*. As well as *taureau* (bull) beef, which is usually served in a rich stew, the Camargue produces a dozen different varieties of rice and the unique *pomme de terre des sables*, a potato grown in sandy soil which is traditionally served

in a salad dressed with olive oil and anchovies from Collioure. Sète's signature dish is *bourride*, a stew of seafood served with garlic-flavoured mayonnaise, while Mèze, on the inner shore of the shallow Bassin de Thau, is well known for its array of seafood – not just oysters, but clams, cockles,

Fresh produce at a local market

mussels, shrimp, crab and lobster, all of which feature in the seafood platters served in its quayside restaurants.

The highland areas of Haut-Languedoc and the Pyrénées are sheep- and goat-rearing country, and produce a delicious choice of locally made goat's cheese. These high, arid uplands also produce fine honeys, each variation of which is redolent of the aromatic herbs, wild flowers and flowering trees close to the hives. Lavender honey from the Uzège and chestnut honey from the Cévennes and the Montagne Noire are among the most distinctive, but local beekeepers produce hundreds of different varieties, no two of which taste quite the same. Connoisseurs say the flavour changes from season to season and even from jar to jar, depending on where the bees have harvested their pollen.

A vineyard near Caunes-Minervois

The combination of hot summer sun and plentiful rainfall makes the whole region perfect for fruit growing. Céret, in the foothills of the Pyrénées, earns its name from the *cerises* (cherries) which flourish in its mellow microclimate and are harvested as early as Easter. Nîmes has its distinctive *gariguette* and *ciflorette* strawberries, while the Cévennes and the Hérault grow sweet chestnuts and onions in profusion. Apricots, plums and figs also flourish in late summer and autumn.

Drinks

The most commonly cultivated fruit is, of course, the grape. Vineyards cover vast swathes of Languedoc-Roussillon. The Aude, Minervois, Hérault and Corbières winegrowing regions of the Pays d'Oc have traditionally produced vast quantities of quaffable, affordable but undistinguished *vins de table* and *vins de pays*. They still do, but in recent years there has been a growing trend towards producing high-quality wines that are truly worthy of their AOC (Appellation d'Origine Contrôlée) status. These are predominantly robust reds, made from Cabernet-Sauvignon, Shiraz and Merlot grapes, but there's also plenty of eminently drinkable rosé to be found.

Beer drinkers will find that their choices are limited in most places to

Carcassonne's shady Bar Felix

Eating out

Places to eat and drink in the region include half a dozen restaurants with one or two Michelin stars, all of which are located in or near the region's main towns and cities. Every town or village has at least one eating-place where you can be sure of a very pleasant lunch or dinner, and at the lower end of the budget range there are plenty of small brasseries where the menu may be limited but the options on offer are both tasty and affordable. There are very few specialist vegetarian restaurants, and meat-free options are a bit limited in most restaurants, so self-catering (*see opposite*) makes sense for purist vegetarians and vegans (*see below*), who will find a mouth-watering choice of fruit and vegetables in all the local produce markets.

The best seafood restaurants, naturally, are on the quaysides of fishing harbours such as Sète, Mèze and Collioure, where you can watch the

undistinguished bottled or keg lager beers which quench a thirst but lack character, though a few fake-Irish 'pubs' serve a wider choice of imported ales.

Water is considered an essential accompaniment to any meal in France, and Languedoc-Roussillon produces several highly rated natural mineral waters. The most famous of these is the naturally sparkling Perrier, from a source near Nîmes, while other well-known *eaux de source* (spring waters) include La Salvetat and Vernière in the Haut-Languedoc, Alet-les-Bains, Sémillante and Quézac. To connoisseurs, each of these has a distinctive taste, influenced by the geology of its source.

EATING OUT ETIQUETTE: SMOKING AND TIPPING

Smoking is prohibited in the indoor areas of all bars, cafés, restaurants and other public spaces, including the public areas of hotels. It is, however, permitted at outdoor tables, although it is increasingly disapproved of almost everywhere.

In terms of tipping, a service charge is generally automatically added to your bill, but in smaller bars, restaurants and cafés, leaving some small change is appreciated, if not essential. In larger, more formal restaurants, an additional cash tip of around 10 per cent is the norm.

boats come in to unload their catch before sitting down to a fine fish lunch.

Self-catering

For those planning a self-catering holiday, local produce markets offer a very wide choice of fresh fruit and vegetables (many of which are organically grown – seek out products labelled as '*bio*'), herbs, cheeses, honey and locally made *charcuterie*. Big supermarkets on the outskirts of all the region's towns make shopping for food a breeze, and British self-caterers will find staples such as HP Sauce, Marmite, Heinz baked beans and PG Tips shelved alongside Mexican, Chinese and Indian foodstuffs in the *exotique* section of most big stores. For self-catering made easy, seek out *traiteur* shops which sell home-cooked, ready-made meals that only need reheating. There's at least one of these in every town and in larger villages.

Food and drink

An *épicerie* colourfully advertises its fresh produce

Entertainment

Opera, ballet, flamenco, Catalan-influenced folk music, French pop and rock, world music, jazz and the re-created tunes of medieval troubadours all flourish in Languedoc-Roussillon. In summer, the region hosts a number of world-class music festivals, and in the August saison des fêtes almost every village, no matter how small, hosts its own open-air one-night festival of music and dancing for young and old.

There are also music bars to suit all tastes in all the larger towns, and Montpellier has a thriving club scene fuelled by its large student community.

In summer, most **village events** are held outdoors, in the village square or in a convenient green space, and the village hall is the main venue in wet or winter weather for musical performances and dances. At smaller village level, most of the musical entertainment is provided by home-grown bands who travel a circuit through the small towns and villages of

The ever-popular Opéra de la Comédie in Montpellier

the region and play a medley of vintage rock, French pop and old-time dance music designed to appeal to all age groups. Village events attract everyone from toddlers to grandparents, and visitors are made welcome.

Travelling circuses tour the region in the summer season, and these range from full-scale operations with acrobats, clowns, tightrope-walkers and exotic animal acts, which visit the larger towns, to small family troupes which play the village halls and may comprise no more than a couple of clowns, a juggler and a trained poodle.

The large **holiday parks** on the Mediterranean coast offer an organised nightly programme of entertainment every night, with shows and dancing for children, teenagers and adults, so for families looking for a lively holiday, these big complexes are a good bet.

Montpellier is the regional hub for more highbrow performances, with its grand Opéra de la Comédie and Opéra

Les Arènes in Nîmes is a popular venue

Berlioz, both of which host performances of opera and classical music by leading ensembles, as well as visiting rock, jazz and pop acts. The city also has a plethora of music bars, and a parade of larger, late-night dance clubs and discos along the Route de Palavas on the city's eastern outskirts. **Béziers** has its own landmark venue, the florid Théâtre Municipal Molière, which provides a stage for theatre, classical music and jazz. Nearby, **Villeneuve-les-Béziers** prides itself on its summer-long programme of *fêtes* and music festivals, starting at the beginning of July and carrying on every weekend until the beginning of September, with Latin and country music, jazz and more in the town's main square. Not far from Carcassonne, the glorious 12th-century **Abbaye de Villelongue** hosts a summer season of classical music and dinner-concerts. Languedoc-Roussillon's most venerable entertainment venue, however, is **Nîmes' Les Arènes**, the Roman arena which provides a venue for performances of all kinds, with space for up to 20,000 spectators.

WHAT'S ON WHEN?

To find out what's on and when, look at the listings pages of the main regional newspaper, *Midi-Libre*, visit the Languedoc-Roussillon Tourist Board website (*www.en.sunfrance.com*), or pick up an events guide from the local Tourist Board office (these are generally published monthly or bi-monthly, and in several languages, including English). In smaller villages, there is usually a noticeboard outside the *mairie* (town hall) or the local *syndicat d'initiative* (information centre) where you'll find fliers advertising upcoming events in the area.

Shopping

Languedoc-Roussillon's boutiques, craft shops, artists' galleries, specialist food shops, produce markets and superstores have enough to satisfy the most demanding shopper. Montpellier has trendy designer shops and fashion boutiques, while potters, painters, silversmiths, weavers and wood-carvers sell some striking and original products from studios in surprisingly remote places. For everyday needs, there are large superstores on the outskirts of all major towns, and smaller ones in town centres.

Superstore chains such as Intermarché, Leclerc and Géant sell everything from baby products to fishing and camping equipment, as well as all kinds of food and drink, toys, clothes and hardware. These are usually located out of town, and most of them also have a petrol station, so you can fill your tank after doing your shopping. Smaller supermarkets such as Monoprix can be found in the centre of most towns. They sell a slightly smaller range, but can still supply most everyday necessities.

While these modern stores are great for one-stop shopping, an essential part of a great holiday in Languedoc-Roussillon is visiting the **local produce markets**. In most towns, these are open on two or three weekdays, but are always at their best on Saturday morning. Here, you can shop for the best seasonal products and local produce – always fresh and often organically produced. For those who are self-catering, the local market will provide herbs, oil, olives, and all the ingredients for an authentic Occitan meal. Most produce markets are in full swing by 8am and the fun is over by midday, when the stalls are folded up, the rubbish is whisked away and the market square is swept clean.

Camargue costume shop in Aigues-Mortes

Markets and supermarkets aside, Languedoc-Roussillon is still a region of small **specialist shops**: by choice, locals buy meat from the butcher, sausage and cold cuts from the *charcutier*, cheese from the cheese shop, fish from the fishmonger and fresh bread from the bakery. Other specialist shops deal in olive oil and herbs, soaps and perfumes, and fruit and vegetables, and it is taken for granted that their stock is a cut above supermarket produce. All over the region, small shops specialise in *produits du terroir*, the local delicacies of their area. These can include goat's cheese, wild-boar sausage, cured ham, olive oil, ceps and more, depending on the region and the season.

Shops known as **brocantes** specialise in second-hand and vintage items of all

EMPTYING THE ATTIC

The *vide-grenier* (literally 'attic-emptying') is a local institution. It's the equivalent of a car boot sale, when local residents display piles of unwanted possessions on trestle tables in the village square and nearby streets in the hope of making a small profit. Much of what is displayed is, of course, just junk, but it's fun to rummage through the heaps of old china, unmatched cutlery, brass candlesticks, chipped glassware and even rusted swords and muskets in the hope of finding an authentic antique. Summer is the season for *vide-grenier*, and you'll see roadside posters advertising them a couple of weeks ahead.

kinds, and may even turn up occasional genuine antiques. For serious antique shoppers there are a few high-quality (and expensive) dealers in Montpellier and Nimes.

Plenty of shops sell colourful souvenirs and local handicrafts

Sport and leisure

For a sporting holiday, Languedoc-Roussillon is simply unbeatable. With terrain that ranges from windswept beaches to rushing rivers, snow-capped peaks to rugged mountains and wooded hill country to gentle lowlands, there's something for everyone here, whether you are a fan of rugby, tennis and golf or prefer the less structured pursuits of mountaineering, kayaking, windsurfing, riding, hill-walking, cycling or – in the Pyrénées in the winter months – skiing.

The region's favourite spectator and participatory sports are **rugby** and **cycling**, while Languedoc also shares the French national passion for **boules**, which is played everywhere. Narbonne is the region's rugby capital, but there are smaller clubs in many towns and villages. The world's greatest cycle race, the Tour de France, is routed through Languedoc-Roussillon most years, and seeing the *peloton* of cyclists hurtling along country roads at high speed is an unforgettable experience.

There are municipal **tennis courts** where you can turn up and play in all

Rugby is the top regional spectator sport

cities and major towns and many villages, and most towns also have their own municipal open-air **swimming pool**.

Many visitors are more than content to spend their leisure time on the beach, by the pool or picnicking by a cool mountain lake, but Languedoc-Roussillon is above all an active holiday destination, with a huge choice of holiday adventures which are readily accessible to all.

Near the coast resorts, several adventure parks such as **Leucate Aventures** (*tel: 0610 04 58 50; www.leucate-aventures.com*) offer an exciting range of activities including treetop wire rides, canyoning and rafting. **Riding** holidays are popular in the Camargue and the Montagne Noire, where you can ride for a day or half-day or make a longer trip along forest trails. There are **walking trails** to suit walkers of all kinds, from demanding hikes in Haut-Languedoc and the high Pyrénées to

Canoeing down the River Orb is a popular pastime for tourists and locals

easy-going strolls along the towpaths of the Canal du Midi.

The breezes of the Mediterranean coast have turned Montpellier into one of Europe's wind- and watersports capitals, and the **Mondial du Vent** (*www.mondial-du-vent.com*) attracts the world's champion windsurfers and kite-surfers to perform amazing stunts every year in mid-April. The flat sandy strands around Narbonne-Plage are also an ideal spot for *chars à voile* (sand-yachting), with tuition and three-wheeled *chars* for hire. **Catamarans** and sailing dinghies can be hired at all the seaside resorts, while for more leisurely days out on the water small day-cruisers can be hired at the leisure harbours which are strategically located along the Canal du Midi.

Places such as Limoux, Arques, Alès and Roquebrun, located on fast-flowing rivers, are popular bases for a whole assortment of exciting activities including **kayaking**, **canoeing**, **hydrospeed** and **river-rafting**. For those who like to get high, mountaineering is popular in the rugged Corbières, with bases at Tautavel, Font-Romeu and Saint-Paul-de-Fenouillet. The Pyrenean slopes at Les Angles also offer **skiing** and **snowboarding** in winter, with even better winter sports just across the border in Andorra.

But Languedoc-Roussillon offers gentler leisure pursuits too. Its therapeutic springs have been known since Roman times, and traditional **spa centres** include Amélie-les-Bains with its large Roman baths, Alet-les-Bains with its natural hot-water swimming pool, the modern La Chaldette mountain thermal centre at Brion, and almost a dozen more scattered throughout the region.

Consult the **Languedoc-Roussillon Tourist Board** website for details and listings of what's on offer (*tel: (0467) 20 02 20; http://en.sunfrance.com*).

Children

Languedoc-Roussillon could have been designed for families, with a super summer climate which is usually neither too hot nor too cold, plenty of family-friendly places to stay, and a vast assortment of purpose-built visitor attractions, including wildlife parks and zoos, aquaparks, adventure centres, and heritage attractions that bring the region's rich history to life in an entertaining way. Children are accepted almost everywhere, and most attractions offer free admission for toddlers and reduced prices for under 12s.

Many restaurants offer a set children's menu, but the choices tend to be limited. *Steak haché* (burger) and chips, pizza, omelette or chicken are the standard offers, usually with ice cream to follow. If these fail to satisfy, the familiar golden arches of a certain multinational fast-food chain can be found in all the main cities, but a self-catering holiday is most likely to keep both children and parents content.

For places to stay, eat, drink and entertain, there are three obvious choices for families. The large **holiday parks** which line the southern part of the Mediterranean coastline offer accommodation in comfortable, modern, self-catering chalets and mobile homes, with swimming pools and water slides for adults, children and toddlers, all-day supervised activities for children of all ages, watersports and beaches with trained lifeguards on duty, and evening entertainment. On-site restaurants, bars and supermarkets mean that all family needs are provided for without having to

leave the site, but nearby can be exciting visitor attractions such as **Dinoland** (*www.dinolandpark.com*) near Cap d'Agde, with its animated dinosaurs, amusement parks and games such as mini-golf, **Europark** (*www.europarkvias.com*) at Vias Plage, **Pirat' Parc** (*tel: (0468) 49 52 96; www.pirat-parc.com*) at Gruissan, with pirate-themed rides and firework displays, or the **Réserve Africaine de Sigean** (*see p60*) at Sigean, with thousands of exciting wild animals as well as cute smaller ones and a petting zoo for younger children.

For families who prefer a more tranquil holiday environment than the bustling Mediterranean coast, there are numerous **campsites** in the lush green hinterland of Haut-Languedoc. These offer a choice of pre-pitched tents and self-catering cabins as well as pitches for independent campers, and many are located by lakes which provide safe beaches, swimming and watersports.

Stalactites and stalagmites in the Grotte de Limousis will wow the children

The best choice of all for those with little ones is a *gîte* with a pool, and these can be found all over the region (*see 'Accommodation', pp164–87*). Some sit in splendid isolation, but there are plenty within walking or cycling distance of villages with cafés, shops and other services.

While the coast excels at providing thrills-and-spills family attractions, the region's hinterland is also well stocked with things to do with children. There are quirky animal attractions and activities such as the **Vallée des Tortues** (*tel: 0674 18 92 11; www.lavalleedestortues.fr*) and its collection of tortoises ranging from ancient giants to cute, tiny hatchlings, the lively **Parc Australien** (*see pp100–101*) near Carcassonne, or family walks with the **Lamas de la Montagne Noire** (*see p113*). For older children and teenagers there are river-based activities such as kayaking and canoeing with **Grandeur Naturel Canoe** in Roquebrun (*see pp121–3*) on the Orb river. Hills and mountains are riddled with impressive caverns such as the vast **Grotte de Limousis** (*see pp112–13*) and the **Gouffre Géant de Cabrespine** (*see p112*), where underground lakes, glittering crystal formations and giant stalactites will fascinate children of all ages.

Many towns have a summer 'mini-train' which makes a circuit of all the local sights and attractions, and these are perfect for sightseeing with smaller children, or just for getting to and from the beach.

Essentials

Arriving and departing

By air

Within Languedoc-Roussillon, there are international airports at Carcassonne, Montpellier, Nîmes and Perpignan, all with flights from the UK and elsewhere in Europe. Just outside the region's boundaries, there are also airports at Toulouse (which is convenient for those planning a holiday in western Languedoc) and Girona in Spain (which is an option for travellers to the Pyrénées-Orientales).

Ryanair (*www.ryanair.com*) flies to Carcassonne from Leeds, Liverpool, Stansted, Nottingham and Prestwick; to Perpignan from Stansted; to Montpellier from Leeds; and to Girona from airports including Birmingham, Bristol, East Midlands, Edinburgh, Prestwick, Leeds, Liverpool, Luton, Gatwick and Stansted.

easyJet (*www.easyjet.com*) flies to Nîmes from Gatwick and to Montpellier from Gatwick and Luton.

By car

Only a very determined driver can complete the 11–12-hour drive from France's northern ferry ports to Languedoc-Roussillon in one day, even on France's excellent *autoroutes*, so it is advisable to plan for an overnight stop at one of the many *villages d'étape* along the way, which specialise in serving long-distance travellers and offer hotels, *pensions, chambres d'hôtes*, restaurants and campsites. An alternative to this is to stay in a no-frills hotel located at one of the motorway junctions. For northeast Languedoc, Nîmes, Montpellier and the Mediterranean coast, the fastest route is the A75 *autoroute* via Clermont-Ferrand. For Carcassonne and the western Languedoc, the best option is the A10/A62/A61 route via Orléans, Limoges and Toulouse. For detailed route planning (including journey times, fuel and *autoroute* toll costs) visit *www.viamichelin.com*

Many stretches of *autoroute* are toll (*péage*) roads, where you take a ticket from a machine on entering and pay on exit. With careful planning, it is possible to avoid *péage* sections by diverting on to the parallel Route Nationale (RN) roads, but this can add several hours to the journey.

The high-speed TGV train

Speed limits are 90km/h (56 mph) on non-motorway roads, 110km/h (68 mph) on non-toll *autoroutes* and 130km/h (80 mph) on toll *autoroutes*. Lower speed limits apply on wet roads.

By train

The fastest way to get to Languedoc-Roussillon by train is to take **Eurostar**'s direct service (in summer only) from London St Pancras International to Avignon (four or five hours' journey time), then connect with an onward SNCF French Railways **TGV** (*www.voyages-sncf.com*) high-speed service to Nîmes, Montpellier, Narbonne or Perpignan. It is also possible to take Eurostar (*tel: 08432 186 186; www.eurostar.com*) to Lille or Paris for onward TGV connections to all these cities (eight to ten hours' journey time).

Customs

France is an EU member and there are in practice no customs formalities for travellers from other EU countries, though vehicles may occasionally be inspected in random security checks and searches for drugs or illegal migrants. Visitors from outside the EU can bring in a litre of spirits, 4 litres of wine, 16 litres of beer and 200 cigarettes (50 cigars or 250 grams of rolling tobacco). Check with your home country's customs authorities to find out how much you can bring back from France.

CONVERSION TABLE

FROM	TO	MULTIPLY BY
Inches	Centimetres	2.54
Feet	Metres	0.3048
Yards	Metres	0.9144
Miles	Kilometres	1.6090
Acres	Hectares	0.4047
Gallons	Litres	4.5460
Ounces	Grams	28.35
Pounds	Grams	453.6
Pounds	Kilograms	0.4536
Tons	Tonnes	1.0160

To convert back, for example, from centimetres to inches, divide by the number in the third column.

MEN'S SUITS

UK	36	38	40	42	44	46	48
Rest of Europe	46	48	50	52	54	56	58
USA	36	38	40	42	44	46	48

DRESS SIZES

UK	8	10	12	14	16	18
France	36	38	40	42	44	46
Italy	38	40	42	44	46	48
Rest of Europe	34	36	38	40	42	44
USA	6	8	10	12	14	16

MEN'S SHIRTS

UK	14	14.5	15	15.5	16	16.5	17
Rest of Europe	36	37	38	39/40	41	42	43
USA	14	14.5	15	15.5	16	16.5	17

MEN'S SHOES

UK	7	7.5	8.5	9.5	10.5	11
Rest of Europe	41	42	43	44	45	46
USA	8	8.5	9.5	10.5	11.5	12

WOMEN'S SHOES

UK	4.5	5	5.5	6	6.5	7
Rest of Europe	38	38	39	39	40	41
USA	6	6.5	7	7.5	8	8.5

Electricity

France uses a 220-volt, 50-cycle AC supply. Plugs have two round pins. UK appliances can use this supply, but require an adapter. These can be bought in some French supermarkets and are also sold at all UK airports and in shops on board ferries.

Internet

Most towns and villages have at least one Internet café (mainly patronised by local youths playing online games). Most modern chain hotels offer free Wi-Fi connection in their public areas, and there are also Wi-Fi hotspots at most airports and at some motorway service stations. The McDonald's fast-food restaurants also offer free Wi-Fi.

Money

France uses the euro, which is divided into 100 cents. Coins are in denominations of 1c, 2c, 5c, 10c, 20c, 50c, and 1 and 2 euros. Notes are in 5, 10, 20, 50, 100 and 500 euro denominations (in practice, 500 euro notes are only used for large cash transactions and some traders are reluctant to accept them). There are ATMS in all but the smallest villages. Major currencies can be changed at all banks, but restricted bank opening hours mean using an ATM is a quicker, easier and more flexible option. Mastercard and Visa credit cards and Visa debit cards using chip-and-PIN are widely accepted in most shops, restaurants and hotels. American Express is less widely accepted, but can be used at most larger hotels and for tourist services such as car rental.

Opening hours

Banks are usually open 9.30am–12.30pm and 2–4pm Monday–Friday. **Petrol stations** are often unstaffed at weekends and from noon to 2pm and accept only automatic credit card payment at these times. This can cause problems for non-French drivers, as some machines will accept only French credit cards, so it is best to avoid running low on fuel at weekends. *Autoroute* service stations, however, are staffed 24 hours daily. **Pharmacies** normally open 9am–1.30pm and 2.30–6pm Monday–Friday and 9am–1.30pm Saturday. **Post offices** are normally open 9am–6pm but in smaller villages often close from noon to 2pm. **Shops**' opening hours in Languedoc-Roussillon are much more restrictive than in the UK, with most shops opening at 9am and closing at 6pm, and shutting for lunch between 1 and 2pm. Some take a two-hour break between noon and 2pm. Many shops also close on Saturday afternoons and most are also closed all day Sunday. Large supermarkets stay open all day until 8pm or 9pm Monday–Saturday and many also open on Sunday.

Passports and visas

Visitors from the UK need only a passport to enter France and may stay indefinitely. Travellers from Australia, Canada, New Zealand, South Africa and the USA do not need a visa, but are limited to a 90-day stay. In theory, visitors from these countries must apply for a *carte de séjour* (resident's permit) and show evidence of funds in order to stay longer. In practice, those planning a longer stay may find it easier to simply pop across the border to Spain, then return for another 90-day sojourn.

Pharmacies

There are pharmacies in all towns and large villages, marked by a prominent green cross. Pharmacists dispense some medicines (such as antibiotics) without a doctor's prescription and can also provide basic first aid. Conversely, a number of off-the-shelf remedies (such as painkillers) that are available everywhere in the UK can be bought only in pharmacies in France. A list of chemists operating outside normal hours is displayed at every pharmacy.

Post

Post offices (La Poste) are signposted by a bright yellow sign and can be found in all but the smallest villages. Postboxes are also yellow. Larger post offices sell stamps from automatic machines which weigh your letter or parcel and dispense stamps accordingly. Stamps (*timbres*) can also be bought in a *tabac* (tobacconist).

Public holidays

1 January – Jour de l'An (New Year's Day)

March/April – Pâques (Easter Sunday and Monday)

1 May – Fête du Travail (May Day/ Labour Day)

8 May – Victoire 1945 (VE Day)

40th day after Easter – L'Ascension (Ascension Thursday)

7th Sunday after Easter – Pentecôte (Whit Sunday and Monday)

14 July – Fête Nationale (Bastille Day)

15 August – L'Assomption (Assumption)

1 November – La Toussaint (All Saints' Day)

11 November – Jour d'Armistice (Remembrance Day)

25 December – Noël (Christmas Day)

Smoking

Smoking is prohibited in all indoor public spaces, including bars, cafés and restaurants, and on public transport. Hotels may offer bedrooms in which smoking is permitted.

Suggested reading and media

Notes from Languedoc (Rupert Wright) is an entertaining account of a British expatriate's travels and experiences in the region.

Labyrinth (Kate Mosse) is an enjoyable historical-conspiracy novel inspired by the 'mysteries' of the Cathars and Rennes-le-Château.

For those interested in the history of the Cathars and the Albigensian

Crusades, *The Perfect Heresy* (Stephen O'Shea), *Massacre at Montségur* (Zoé Oldenbourg), *The Cathars* (Sean Martin) and *Montaillou* (Emmanuel Le Roy Ludence) are all highly readable.

A few bookshops – at least one in each of the major towns – stock English books and newspapers, which generally go on sale the day after publication in the UK. There are also English-language bookshops at Carcassonne, Nîmes, Montpellier and Perpignan airports, and newsagents in main railway stations also sell British newspapers.

There are no local English-language newspapers, but *The Languedoc Page*

St-Pons' unusually picturesque public toilet

(*www.the-languedoc-page.com*), a website aimed at British expatriates, has forums, blogs and a newsletter, and also offers online travel bookings.

Tax

A TVA (VAT) tax of 19.6 per cent is added to most purchases in France. Visitors from non-EU countries can claim a rebate on certain expensive purchases. Ask in stores for details.

Telephones

Public payphones can be found at main railway stations, airports, and in main post offices. Coin-operated phones have been phased out in most places, but where they are still found (in some hotels and cafés) they take 10c, 20c, 50c and 1 euro coins. Phonecards (*télécartes*) in denominations of €5 and €10 can be bought from branches of Orange and its competitor Bouygues, as well as in some tabacs and post offices. Credit and debit cards can also be used. Mobile phone coverage is generally adequate, but can be poor in remoter mountain areas. Mobile phones use the GSM system and some phones bought outside Europe may not work in France.

The country code for France is *33*. Telephone numbers throughout Languedoc-Roussillon start with *04*, followed by a two-digit *département* code. Mobile numbers start with *06*. Numbers beginning *0800*, *0804*, *0805* or *0809* are free to call from landlines; charges vary for other *08* numbers.

Time

France is one hour ahead of Greenwich Mean Time and six to nine hours ahead of the USA.

Toilets

Public toilets can be found at railway and bus stations and at airports. Most are free. Not all have wheelchair access. Coin-operated public toilets can be found in some cities. These are cleaned automatically. Public toilets in smaller villages and in some bars and cafés are often old-fashioned 'squatter' affairs and may be rather dirty; toilet paper is rarely supplied.

Travellers with disabilities

Wheelchair users are not very well served in France, though accessibility is improving, with more wheelchair ramps and better access to public transport. Many taxis are accessible, as are all airports, but buses and many trains are less easy to use. Modern hotels and holiday camps are all wheelchair-friendly, but smaller pensions and guesthouses often have steep stairs and no lift. The **Association des Paralyses de France** (*tel: (0467) 10 03 25; www.apf.asso.fr*), with a regional office in Montpellier, provides a list of wheelchair-accessible accommodation.

Montpellier transport map

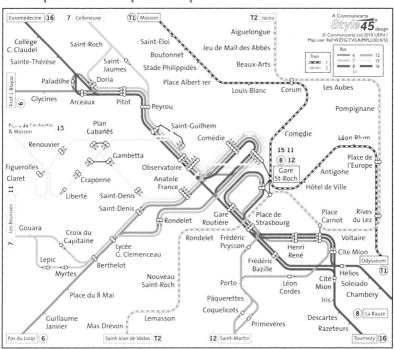

Language

English is not widely spoken in Languedoc-Roussillon, except in large hotels and by staff at tourist offices and airports. Road signs often feature traditional Occitan place names as well as the modern French version or, near the Spanish border, are in both French and Catalan, but neither language is widely spoken, and anyone who does speak Occitan or Catalan will also speak French.

French uses two forms for the word 'you': *vous* is both the plural and the more formal form of address; *tu* or *toi* is more familiar, and is used by adults to children and between close friends. Until you know someone well, use the *vous* form. To use *tu/toi* inappropriately is considered presumptuous, and there is even a verb for it: *tutoyer*. People are always addressed as Monsieur (Sir/Mr), Madame (Madam/Mrs) or Mademoiselle (Miss).

Please	S'il vous plaît	**Good morning**	Bonjour
Thank you	Merci	**Good afternoon**	Bon après-midi
Excuse me	Pardon/Excusez-moi	**Good evening**	Bonsoir/Bonne soirée
Yes	Oui		
No	Non	**Good night**	Bonne nuit
How are you?	Comment allez-vous?	**Goodbye**	Au revoir
		Today	Aujour d'hui
How much?	Combien?	**Tomorrow**	Demain
I do not understand	Je ne comprends pas	**Yesterday**	Hier
		Morning	Matin
Speak less quickly, please	S'il vous plaît, parlez moins vite	**Noon**	Midi
		Afternoon	Après-midi
Do you speak English?	Parlez-vous anglais?	**Evening**	Soir
		Night	Nuit
Hello	Bonjour		

Sunday	Dimanche	**January**	Janvier	**July**	Juillet
Monday	Lundi	**February**	Fevrier	**August**	Août
Tuesday	Mardi	**March**	Mars	**September**	Septembre
Wednesday	Mercredi	**April**	Avril	**October**	Octobre
Thursday	Jeudi	**May**	Mai	**November**	Novembre
Friday	Vendredi	**June**	Juin	**December**	Décembre
Saturday	Samedi				

One	Un/Une	Twelve	Douze	Forty	Quarante
Two	Deux	Thirteen	Treize	Fifty	Cinquante
Three	Trois	Fourteen	Quatorze	Sixty	Soixante
Four	Quatre	Fifteen	Quinze	Seventy	Soixante-dix
Five	Cinq	Sixteen	Seize	Eighty	Quatre-vingt
Six	Six	Seventeen	Dix-sept		
Seven	Sept	Eighteen	Dix-huit	Ninety	Quatre-vingt-dix
Eight	Huit	Nineteen	Dix-neuf		
Nine	Neuf	Twenty	Vingt	Hundred	Cent
Ten	Dix	Thirty	Trente	Thousand	Mille
Eleven	Onze				

Airport	Aéroport	Mineral water	Eau minerale
Bus station	Gare routière	Sparkling water	Eau gazeuse
Railway station	Gare	Beer	Bière
Single/return ticket	Aller simple/retour	Wine	Vin
Ticket office	Billetterie	Bread	Pain
Shuttle bus	Navette	Cheese	Fromage
Car	Voiture	Ham	Jambon
Car park	Parking	Chicken	Poulet
Petrol	Essence	Vegetables	Légumes
Motorway	Autoroute	Breakfast	Petit déjeuner
Map	Carte	Lunch	Déjeuner
Boat	Bateau	Dinner	Dîner
I would like to rent a car/bicycle	Je veux louer une voiture/bicyclette	Where?	Où?
		When?	Quand?
		Why?	Pourquoi?
A room for one/two	Une chambre pour une personne/deux personnes	How?	Comment?
		How much?	Combien?
		How far?	C'est à quelle distance?
Bathroom	Salle de bain		
Toilet	Toilette	How long?	Combien de temps?
Shower	Douche		
Beach	Plage	Enough	Assez
Hot	Chaud	Too much	Trop
Cold	Froid	Cheap	Bon marché
Bakery	Boulangerie	Good	Bon
Grocer	Épicerie	Bad	Mal/Mauvais
Butcher	Boucherie		
Coffee	Café		
Tea	Thé		

Emergencies

Emergency numbers
European all-emergency number (from mobile phones) *112*
Fire brigade *18*
Medical emergencies *15*
Police *17*
Sea, lake or river rescue *1616*

Medical services
Doctors and dentists
There are doctors and dentists in all major towns and cities and in larger villages.

Hospitals
There are major hospitals providing full accident and emergency services in Béziers, Carcassonne, Montpellier, Narbonne, Nîmes and Perpignan:
Béziers *Centre Hospitalier de Béziers. 2 rue Valentin Haug. Tel: (0467) 35 70 35. www.ch-beziers.fr*
Carcassonne *Centre Hospitalier de Carcassonne. Tel: (0468) 24 24 24. www.ch-carcassonne.fr*
Montpellier *Centre Hospitalier Universitaire de Montpellier. Tel: (0467) 63 38 25. www.chu-montpellier.fr*
Narbonne *Centre Hospitalier de Hôtel-Dieu. 10 rue Henri Dunant. Tel: (0468) 42 60 00. www.ch-narbonne.fr*
Nîmes *Centre Hospitalier Universitaire. 4 avenue Professeur*

Robert Debre. Tel: (0466) 68 68 68. www.chu-nimes.fr
Perpignan *Centre Hospitalier de Perpignan. 57 avenue Victor Dalbiez. Tel: (0468) 85 72 00. www.ch-perpignan.fr*

Opticians
Opticians providing replacement prescription glasses, contact lenses and frame repair can be found in all main towns and in many larger villages. Opticians can usually be found within larger hypermarket complexes also, such as Géant, Intermarché and Leclerc.

Pharmacies
There are numerous pharmacies in all towns and larger villages, indicated by a neon green cross sign. Pharmacies provide basic first aid and medication including some antibiotics.

Prescription medication
Travellers who require prescription medication should make sure they bring an adequate supply, as French pharmacies are unlikely to be able to fill a foreign prescription and usually require a prescription from a French doctor, who will charge a fee for an examination and a prescription.

Health and accident insurance
Health and accident insurance is advisable (and essential for non-EU visitors). The European EHIC card

entitles EU citizens to a basic level of care in France, but many treatments must be paid for.

Visitors planning to take part in adventure activities such as kayaking, canoeing, mountaineering, scuba diving and other sports should make sure they are covered for possible injuries.

Health risks

There are no special health risks in Languedoc-Roussillon, though visitors should beware of sunburn and possible heat exhaustion during the hottest months, when temperatures have been known to reach almost 40°C (104°F). A variety of biting and stinging insects are present in summer, and using mosquito repellent may be advisable in some areas. One species of venomous snake, the adder or viper, is not uncommon but is not aggressive. Its bite is unlikely to prove dangerous, but anyone bitten should seek medical advice immediately.

Gathering wild edible fungi is a favourite autumn pastime in the region. However, if you are planning on doing this, you should be very sure that you can identify edible species and avoid poisonous varieties. If in any doubt, consult a pharmacy, as they offer a free fungus identification service.

Safety and crime

Languedoc-Roussillon does not generally have a reputation for violent crime, but petty theft is not uncommon and thieves often target isolated holiday homes and foreign cars. Make sure that valuables are concealed or locked away when you are away from your holiday home. It's also a good idea to use hotel safes or security boxes if they're available, and never leave cameras or other valuables within sight in a parked car – lock them in the boot.

Embassies and consulates

There are no embassies in Languedoc-Roussillon. Paris contact details are listed below:

Australian Embassy
4 rue Jean Rey, 15e.
Tel: (01) 40 59 33 00.
www.france.embassy.gov.au

British Embassy
35 rue du Faubourg Saint-Honoré, Concorde. Tel: (01) 44 51 31 00.
http://ukinfrance.fco.gov.uk

Canadian Embassy
35 avenue Montaigne.
Tel: (01) 44 43 29 00
www.canadainternational.gc.ca/france

New Zealand Embassy
7 rue Léonard de Vinci, 16e.
Tel: (01) 45 01 43 43.
www.nzembassy.com/france

South African Embassy
59 quai d'Orsay, 7e.
Tel: (01) 53 59 23 23.
www.afriquesud.net

US Embassy
2 avenue Gabriel, Concorde.
Tel: (01) 43 12 22 22.
http://france.usembassy.gov

Directory

Accommodation price guide

Prices are per double room per night. Most hotels don't include breakfast in the room rate but offer it for a nominal extra charge (on average around €10), unless otherwise stated.

£	up to €80
££	€81–125
£££	€126–250
££££	over €250

Eating out price guide

The prices listed are based on an average-priced meal for one, without drinks, so you may pay a good deal more or somewhat less than the price shown, depending on your choice of meal.

£	up to €40
££	€40–70
£££	€70–100
££££	over €100

MONTPELLIER, NÎMES AND NORTHERN LANGUEDOC

Aigues-Mortes

ACCOMMODATION

Les Arcades ££

Centrally located and set within a converted 16th-century building, all the nine rooms in this charming 3-star hotel are reached via a sweeping stone spiral staircase and are named after local birds. Despite the historic setting, however, all are spacious, en-suite and air-conditioned. There's also the added bonus of a swimming pool on the rooftop terrace. Breakfast is not included in the price but is available for an extra charge. The hotel restaurant is also locally renowned.
23 boulevard Gambetta, 30220 Aigues-Mortes.
Tel: (0466) 53 81 13.
www.les-arcades.fr

EATING OUT

Les Arcades £

The restaurant of this 3-star hotel has a local reputation for light, modern cuisine, in contrast to the hearty traditional fare of the Camargue which is the staple of many Aigues-Mortes restaurants. Choose from tables in air-conditioned comfort within the 16th-century building, or outside on the terrace, just round the corner from the bustling Place Saint-Louis.
23 boulevard Gambetta.
Tel: (0466) 53 81 13.
www.les-arcades.fr.
Open: Wed, Fri, Sat & Sun noon–3pm & 7–9.30pm, Tue & Thur 7–9.30pm.

Le Café du Commerce £

Although it calls itself a café, this is really a large open-air restaurant on Aigues-Mortes' main square, serving shellfish from the nearby lagoons, *taureau* from the Camargues ranches, and fresh fish from the Sète fleet.

11 place Saint-Louis.
Tel: (0466) 53 71 71.
www.cafeducommerce-
aiguesmortes.com.
Open: Feb Tue–Fri
& Sun noon–2pm, Sat
noon–2pm & 7–9.30pm;
Mar Tue–Sun noon–2pm;
Apr–end Sept Tue–Sun
noon–2pm & 7–9.30pm.
Closed: Nov & Dec.

La Camargue ££

La Camargue is a local
institution. It claims to be
the oldest eating place in
Aigues-Mortes, and its
gypsy musicians and
flamenco dancers attract
the crowds every evening.
Despite its unashamed
appeal to the tourist
traffic, the traditional
camarguais menu is still
worth sampling, and
overall La Camargue lives
up to its reputation.
19 rue de la République.
Tel: (0466) 53 86 88. www.
restaurantlacamargue.com.
Open: noon–2pm &
7–9.30pm.

Casa Toro Luna ££

This Spanish-influenced
restaurant in the main
square is a carnivore's
heaven, specialising in
beef from the Camargue
in all shapes and forms.
Lesser appetites can settle

for *tapas* snacks and the
restaurant also serves an
excellent paella.
Place Saint-Louis.
Open: noon–3pm & 7–
9.30pm. Closed: Jan.

ENTERTAINMENT
La Camargue

Aigues-Mortes' best-
known restaurant is
famous for its gypsy
guitarists and flamenco
dancers. See website for
dates and times of
performances, which take
place most nights in July
and August.
19 rue de la République.
Tel: (0466) 53 86 88.
www.restaurantla
camargue.com. Open:
noon–2pm & 7–9.30pm.

SPORT AND LEISURE
Les Péniches Îsles de Stel

See the lagoons, water-
meadows, salt mountains,
flamingos, bulls and white
horses in comfort from
the upper deck of one of
these purpose-built canal
cruisers which set out
daily from Aigues-Mortes
in summer.
12 rue Amiral Corbet.
Tel: (0466) 53 60 70.
www.islesdestel.camargue.
fr. Admission charge.

Ranch de la Brouzetière

One of several ranches
near Aigues-Mortes
where visitors can meet
and ride the famous
white horses of the
Camargue. La Brouzetière
offers guided riding trips
along the long, empty
beaches or in the
Camargue hinterland,
with mounts suitable
for expert riders,
novices, and even
small children.
Route d'Arlès, Saintes-
Maries-de-la-Mer.
Tel: (0490) 97 82 40. www.
labrouzetiere.camargue.fr.
Open: year-round daily.
Admission charge.

Anduze
SPORT AND LEISURE
Train à Vapeur des Cévennes

This is a spectacular and
enjoyable steam train
journey along one of the
most scenically attractive
stretches of line in
Languedoc-Roussillon.
The timetable allows
travellers to stop off, visit
some sights along the
way and at either end of
the route (such as the
colourful local markets in
Saint-Jean-du-Gard and

Anduze), then re-embark.
38 place du Gare.
Tel: (0466) 60 59 00.
www.trainavapeur.com.
Departures from Anduze:
Apr–mid-May Tue–Sun
11.30am & 3pm; mid-
May–end Sept daily
11.30am, 3pm & 5pm
(but times are subject
to change, so call the
ticket office or visit the
website for updates).
Admission charge.

La Grande-Motte
ACCOMMODATION
Hôtel Azur ££
A beachfront 3-star hotel
with its own pool and
lovely gardens. The en-
suite rooms are a little
bland in their décor
but have private terraces
that look out over either
the sea or the port.
The private carpark is
an added bonus.
Breakfast is available for
an extra charge.
Place Justin.
Tel: (0467) 56 56 00.
www.hotelazur.net

EATING OUT
Alexandre ££
This fine, modern
restaurant beside the
yacht-filled pleasure

port stands head and
shoulders above the
main array of run-of-
the-mill eating places in
this purpose-built
holiday resort.
Esplanade Maurice Justin.
Tel: (0467) 56 63 63. www.
alexandre-restaurant.com.
Open: Jul & Aug Tue–Sun
noon–3pm & 7–10pm; rest
of the year Tue–Sat noon–
3pm & 7–10pm, Sun
noon–3pm. Closed: Mon,
Oct–Mar Tue, & Jan.

Mèze
ACCOMMODATION
Hôtel de la Pyramide ££
On the edge of the
lagoon with views of
sailing boats and
windsurfers is this stylish
hotel. All of the 22 rooms
have private balconies
or terraces, and there's a
lovely pool area and
surrounding gardens of
olive and chestnut trees.
8 promenade Sergent J L
Navarro.
Tel: (0467) 46 61 50.
www.hoteldelapyramide.fr

EATING OUT
La Marmitière ££
Coquillages (shellfish)
from the Bassin de Thau
are the signature dishes

here, but grilled prawns,
fish, lobster and duck all
have their place on the
menu.
38 rue du Port.
Tel: (0467) 43 84 99.
www.lamarmitiere.fr.
Open: daily noon–2pm &
7–10pm.

Montpellier
ACCOMMODATION
Hôtel du Palais £
Located in the old part of
Montpellier, beside the
Peyrou Gardens, is the
elegant façade of the 2-
star Hôtel du Palais. The
whole place is nicely
decorated in pale peach
and lemon shades and all
rooms are en-suite, with
either shower or bath.
On sunny days breakfast
(extra charge) can be
enjoyed at patio tables in
front of the hotel.
3 rue du Palais des
Guilhem.
Tel: (0467) 60 47 38.
www.hoteldupalais-
montpellier.fr
Hotel du Parc £
This small, owner-
operated hotel north of
the historic centre (but
easily accessible by tram,
bus or on foot) is
colourful, relaxed and

amazingly good value. With only 19 rooms within what was originally an 18th-century building, the bedrooms are on the small side, but the lobby and reception area are quite grand, with a winding staircase leading to the upper floors. Modern facilities include wireless Internet hotspot access and free parking (but reserve your parking space in advance, as spots are at a premium).
8 Rue Achille Bégé.
Tel: (0467) 41 16 49.
www.hotelduparc-montpellier.com

Hotel d'Aragon ££

This is a small and surprisingly elegant townhouse hotel, handy for both the historic charms of Montpellier and for the city's mainline railway station, which is only 500m (541yds) away. The rooms range from large and comfortable doubles and twins to 'privilege hydrojet' suites with whirlpool baths. Buffet breakfast is served in the conservatory-style Verandah café-

restaurant, and facilities include wireless Internet access.
10 Rue Baudin.
Tel: (0467) 10 70 00.
www.hotel-aragon.fr

Hôtel le Guilhem ££

In the historic centre, overlooking the Palais de Justice, is this 16th-century building converted into a pleasant hotel. The elegant rooms – some with garden views, one with exposed stonework – are decorated in traditional style but are all en-suite.
18 rue Jean-Jacques Rousseau.
Tel: (0467) 52 90 90.
www.leguilhem.com

Hotel Kyriad Montpellier Antigone ££

Part of a France-wide chain, but none the worse for that, this medium-sized modern hotel is in the middle of Montpellier's contemporary, idiosyncratic Antigone Quarter. It is a little bland, but has the benefit of being just ten minutes from the airport, just off the *autoroute*, so it is a good spot for a short break or for a first- or

last-night stay for those arriving or leaving from Montpellier by air or rail.
890 Avenue Jean Mermoz.
Tel: (0467) 64 80 50.
www.kyriad-montpelliercentre.com

Hotel Royal ££

This pleasant, slightly chintzy 3-star hotel, with its pink-and-cream colour schemes, claims to be in the heart of Montpellier's historic centre. In fact, it's on the fringe of the old quarter, less than a minute's walk from Place de la Comédie. The railway station is only 100m (110yds) away, and a taxi to the airport takes just 15 minutes, so this is excellently located for a short city break in Montpellier.
8 Rue Maguelone.
Tel: (0467) 92 13 36.
www. royalhotel montpellier.com

EATING OUT

Verdi £

Unassuming, inexpensive pizza and pasta joint a few steps from the main railway station. Also serves good seafood, and has its own wine shop.

10 rue A Olivier.
Tel: (0467) 58 68 55.
Open: Mon–Sat noon–3pm
& 6–10pm. Closed: Sun &
first three weeks in Aug.

Tamarillos ££

Colourful restaurant
noted for its use of ultra-
fresh local organic
produce, and worth
visiting just for its award-
winning, dazzlingly
original dessert menu.
Booking advisable.
2 place Marché aux
Fleures.
Tel: (0467) 60 06 00.
www.tamarillos.biz

Le Jardin des Sens £££

With two Michelin stars,
this is the gourmand's
choice in Montpellier.
North African influences
are evident in dishes
such as pigeon *pastille*
but the menu pays due
homage to the products
of the Languedoc
hinterland and the
Mediterranean.
Booking essential.
11 avenue Saint-Lazare.
Tel: (0499) 58 38 38.
www.jardindessens.com.
Open: Tue & Thur–Sat
noon–2.30pm &
7–9.30pm, Mon & Wed
7–9.30pm. Closed: Sun &
first two weeks in Jan.

ENTERTAINMENT

Cargo

Montpellier's biggest,
liveliest and longest-
established dance club,
music bar and live music
venue.
5 rue du Grand Saint-
Jean. Tel: (0467) 29 96 85.
www.cargo-montpellier.fr.
Open: Tue–Thur 8pm–
2am, Fri & Sat 8pm–
5am. Closed: Sun & Mon.
Admission charge for
some events.

JAM

Jazz Action Montpellier
is a vibrant venue for
more than 100 concerts
every year, concentrating
on classic and
contemporary jazz and
world music.
100 rue Ferdinand de
Lesseps. Tel: (0467) 58 30
30. www.lejam.com.
Open: see website or local
listings for performances.
Admission charge for
some events.

Rockstore

Rockstore is a combined
dance club, VIP lounge,
rock café and concert
venue hosting DJs, live
bands and a range of
themed events.
20 rue du Verdun.
Tel: (0467) 06 80 00.

www.rockstore.fr. Open:
every night, hours vary, so
see website or local listings
for times. Admission
charge for some events.

Nîmes

ACCOMMODATION

Hôtel Kyriad £

A good budget option
with a very central
location as well as a
private carpark, which is
not to be scoffed at in
towns such as Nîmes. The
rooms are basic but clean
and are all air-conditioned
and en-suite. Some rooms
have a terrace (for a
slightly higher rate).
10 rue Roussy.
Tel: (0466) 76 16 20. www.
hotel-kyriad-nimes.com

New Hôtel La Baume £££

Nîmes may be noted for
its Roman sights, but this
17th-century house is
rather special, lovingly
converted into an elegant
hotel with vaulted
ceilings and courtyards –
and it's just moments
from Nîmes' main
attractions. The rooms,
though equipped with all
mod cons, are decorated
in keeping with the
history of the building.
21 rue Nationale.

Tel: (0466) 76 28 42.
www.new-hotel.com

EATING OUT

Aux Plaisirs des Halles £

A few steps from the Maison Carrée, this restaurant offers tremendous value for money. There's a leafy terrace for outdoor dining on warm summer evenings, the menu is contemporary and emphasises seasonal produce, and the wine list focuses on the best of Languedoc.

4 rue Littré.
Tel: (0466) 36 01 02. www.auxplaisirsdeshalles.com.
Open: Tue–Sat noon–3pm & 7–10pm. Closed: Sun & Mon & 8–15 Jun.

Le Marché sur la Table £

Next to Aux Plaisir des Halles, this recent arrival on the Nîmes restaurant scene also buys its ingredients fresh every morning from the produce market which is virtually next door. Good bistro-style cooking with a light touch.

10 rue Littré.
Tel: (0466) 67 22 50.
Open: Wed–Sun noon–2pm & 7–10pm.

Le Bouchon et L'Assiette ££

Charming, friendly restaurant serving a combination of contemporary and traditional regional dishes, with a menu that changes according to the season.

5 bis rue de Sauve.
Tel: (0466) 62 02 93.
Open: Thur–Mon noon–2.30pm & 7–10pm.
Closed: Tue, Wed, mid-Jul–mid-Aug & 2–17 Jan.

Le Lisita ££

Olivier Douet offers a fresh take on regional dishes such as *brandade* and *filet de taureau de Camargue*, preluded by seasonal vegetables and cheeses and followed by superb desserts.

Boulevard des Arènes.
Tel: (0466) 67 29 15.
www.lelisita.com. Open: Tue–Sat noon–2pm & 7–9.30pm. Closed: Sun & Mon.

ENTERTAINMENT

Arènes de Nîmes

As well as its notorious bullfights, the ancient Roman arena in the heart of Nîmes is a breathtaking venue for a range of other less gory performances of music, opera and dance as well as sporting events.

1 rue Alexandre Ducros.
Ticket office: 4 rue de la Violette. Tel: 0891 701 401.
www.arenesdenimes.com.
Open: hours vary, so visit the ticket office or website for details. Admission charge.

Le Pont du Gard

EATING OUT

Les Terrasses £

This brasserie has an unbeatable view of the ancient Roman aqueduct but does not over-exploit its monopoly of the location. Its menu is unpretentious but tasty, with plenty of offerings for children and to suit all tastes and budgets – and it's worth eating here just for the view of one of Languedoc-Roussillon's signature sights.

Esplanade Rive Droite.
Tel: (0466) 37 50 88.

Les Saintes-Maries-de-la-Mer

ACCOMMODATION

Camping La Brise £

This campsite is located just outside the lively

summer resort and fishing village of Les Saintes-Maries-de-la-Mer, on the edge of the Camargue. The long sandy beach which stretches away to the east is protected by the Camargue National Park, so there are no other campsites or hotels, making this a great place for a beach-combing holiday. As well as plenty of spaces for self-pitched tents, there are ready-pitched *bungalis* (family tents on wooden decks) and mobile homes. Facilities include a large pool and supervised watersports.
Rue Marcel Carriere.
Tel: (0490) 97 84 67.
www.camping-labrise.fr

Sète
ACCOMMODATION
Grand Hôtel ££
Right on the harbour, you know this is something special as soon as you walk into the impressive marble foyer. The décor throughout has managed to wonderfully blend Baroque-style elements with contemporary features such as stripped

wooden floors and bright colours. Despite all this, it's remarkably good value for such a popular town.
17 quai de Tassigny.
Tel: (0467) 74 71 77.
www.legrandhotelsete.com

Hôtel Port Marine ££
A modern and, frankly, slightly bland hotel, the attraction here is the location, just moments from the harbour and overlooking the sea. Some rooms include a private terrace and there are also apartments, complete with basic kitchen facilities, which are ideal for a longer stay. There's a pool as well as private parking.
Le Môle Saint-Louis.
Tel: (0467) 74 92 34.
http://en-hotel-port-marine.com

EATING OUT
Quai 17 £
The restaurant of the charming old Grand Hôtel, overlooking Sète's prettiest stretch of canal, has a contemporary menu that belies its setting. The dining room is decorated with mural paintings of boats and fishermen, and there

is also an attractive terrace.
17 quai de Tassigny.
Tel: (0467) 74 71 77. www. legrandhotelsete.com.
Open: Mon–Fri noon–2pm & 7–10pm, Sat 7–10pm. Closed: Sun & second half of Jul.

Paris Méditerrannée ££
Competition for the title of best seafood restaurant in Sète is tough, but this establishment is a very strong contender.
47 rue Pierre-Semard.
Tel: (0467) 74 97 74.
Open: Tue–Fri noon–2pm & 7–9.30pm, Sat 7–9.30pm. Closed: Sun & Mon, 1–15 Jul & first week in Feb.

Uzès
EATING OUT
Les 80 Jours
The leafy terrace of this Jules Verne-themed restaurant (the name is inspired by his *Around the World in 80 Days*) is the pleasantest place for lunch on the square in the heart of this postcard-pretty town. The menu is contemporary, with

plenty of affordable offerings – and of course the truffles for which Uzès is famous appear on the menu in season.
2 place Albert 1er.
Tel: (0466) 22 09 89.
Open: Mon–Sat noon–2.30pm & 7–9.30pm.
Closed: Sun & Mon, Nov–Mar & Feb.

BÉZIERS AND NARBONNE
Abbaye de Fontfroide
ENTERTAINMENT
Les Nocturnes de Fontfroide
Actors, musicians and other performers enliven the grounds of the medieval abbey on summer evenings in an astonishing spectacle, combined with dinner in the abbey's restaurant.
Abbaye de Fontfroide,
Tel: (0468) 45 11 08.
www.fontfroide.com.
Performances: Jul & Aug Wed & Thur 10pm.
Admission charge.

Béziers
EATING OUT
La Maison de Campagne £
This bright, spacious, modern restaurant offers amazingly good value, with set menus that will suit any budget. Those with deeper pockets will find that there are some superb gourmet offerings too.
22 avenue Pierre Verdier.
Tel: (0467) 30 91 85.
www.aupauvrejacques.fr.
Open: Tue–Thur noon–2pm, Wed–Sat noon–2pm & 7–9pm. Closed: Sun & Mon, second two weeks in Aug & mid-Dec–end of first week in Jan.

Octopus ££
Dazzlingly original selection of dishes which make the most of the fruits of Languedoc-Roussillon's seas, pastures and fields. The restaurant offers a choice of several different dining rooms, plus (most attractive of all, in summer) a charming outside terrace. The wine list, in contrast to the cosmopolitan influences that are evident in the food menu, focuses on AOCs from the Corbières and the Pays d'Oc.
12 rue Boieldieu.
Tel: (0467) 49 90 00. www. restaurant-octopus.com.
Open: Tue–Sat noon–2pm & 7–9.30pm. Closed: Sun & Mon & mid-Aug–first week in Sept.

L'Ambassade £££
For a special treat or a special occasion, L'Ambassade offers up classic French cooking with a light touch. Expect *foie gras, mousse au homard* (lobster mousse), *crêpes suzettes* and a wine list crammed with some luscious local vintages.
22 boulevard de Verdun.
Tel: (0467) 76 06 24.
Open: Tue–Sat noon–2.30pm & 7–9.30pm.
Closed: Sun & Mon.

Cap d'Agde
ACCOMMODATION
Hôtel du Golfe £££
With its lush gardens, tempting swimming pool and crisp, contemporary design, this 3-star hotel by the sea is an ideal place to stay. There are also gym facilities and a sauna. The rooms are a little unimaginative in their design but some have private terraces. The suites, however, are the very epitome of modern style.
Île des Loisirs.

Tel: (0467) 26 87 03.
www.hotel-du-golf.com

Gruissan
EATING OUT
La Cranquette £
This bistro is a little way inland from Gruissan's busy summer beach, so avoids most of the summer crowds. But it is well worth heading inland for La Cranquette's excellent local seafood, complemented by good meaty grills and an extensive wine list.
10 rue de la République.
Tel: (0468) 75 12 07.
Open: Jul & Aug daily noon–2pm & 7–9.30pm;
Sept–Jun Wed–Sun noon–2pm & 7–9.30pm.

SPORT AND LEISURE
Europlongée
Trial dives, scuba courses, half-day and full-day dive trips, and equipment hire for novices and experienced divers.
Résidence La Farigoule, Quai des Palmiers.
www.euro-plongee.fr.
Open: year-round daily, hours vary so call or visit website for times.
Gruissan Aventure
Gruissan Aventure hires out windsurfing equipment and other watersports kit by the hour or by the day.
Bâtiment H, Résidence Logis de Languedoc.
Tel: (0468) 49 35 74.
Gruissan Kite Passion
Kites and kite-boards for hire in all shapes, sizes and colours, for all ages.
Plage des Salins & 4 rue Pasteur. Tel: 0674 91 94 39.
www.gruissankite passion.com

Narbonne
ACCOMMODATION
Hôtel du Midi £
A smart 2-star in the centre of town, recently renovated in a contemporary style – think blacks and greys with just a hint of accent colour. There's an on-site restaurant and car parking too. Great value for such a location.
4 avenue de Toulouse.
Tel: (0468) 41 04 62.
www.hoteldumidi.net
Camping la Nautique ££
Just off the autoroute, this big camping offers self-catering mobile home accommodation as well as pitches for tents. Close to the inland shores of the Étang de Bages, it has good windsurfing and other water sports on offer. It is also an excellent base for families with children of all ages, from toddlers to teens.
Étang de Bages, exit 38 off A9 autoroute, 4.8 km (3 miles) southwest of Narbonne.
Tel: (0468) 90 48 19. www.campinglanautique.com
La Résidence ££
A charmingly presented 19th-century building converted into a modern-style hotel with crisp white walls, chandelier lighting, sweeping staircase and smart lounge. The rooms are a mix of traditional French style and modern conveniences, and some have views of the town's impressive cathedral. Wine lovers will enjoy the tastings offered of local vintages.
6 rue du 1er Mai.
Tel: (0468) 32 19 41.
www.hotelresidence.fr

EATING OUT
Le 26 £
Good choice of shellfish and seafood, but also some sturdy red-meat

dishes (beef, veal, venison) to delight true carnivores.
8 boulevard du Docteur Lacroix.
Tel: (0468) 41 46 49.
www.restaurantle26.fr.
Open: Mon noon–2pm, Tue–Fri noon–2pm & 7–9pm, Sat 7–9.30pm.
Closed: Sun.

Le Petit Comptoir £
While restaurants all over Languedoc-Roussillon are joining the rush to modernise their ambience and their menus, Le Petit Comptoir remains determinedly retro in terms of its décor and its menu, which places the emphasis on traditional southern dishes, with a wine list that favours domaines from Languedoc-Roussillon and Provence.
4 boulevard Maréchal Joffre. Tel: (0468) 42 30 35. www.petitcomptoir.com.
Open: daily noon–2.30pm & 7–9pm. Closed: last two weeks in Jul & first week in Jan.

La Table Saint-Crescent £££
The finest eating place in Narbonne tempts the palate with inventive juxtapositions of some of the best flavours of Languedoc-Roussillon. Oysters with ham from the Montagne Noire sounds like an unlikely combination, but it works, as do lots of other offerings here.
Palais du Vin, 68 avenue Général Leclerc.
Tel: (0468) 41 37 37. www.la-table-saint-crescent.com

Narbonne-Plage
ACCOMMODATION
Camping La Côte des Roses £
A lakeside campsite with a bar, restaurant and shop, various sports facilities including tennis, basketball and watersports, and easy access to the beach.
Route de Gruissan.
Tel: (0468) 49 83 65.
Open: May–Aug.

Hôtel de la Clape £
Charm and style is not really a feature of accommodation in this area – the key is location, and this hotel is moments away from the beach. The rooms are basic but are all en-suite, and the restaurant has patio tables in summer. There's also a swimming pool if you're tired of having sand between your toes.
4 rue des Fleurs.
Tel: (0468) 49 80 15.
www.hoteldelaclape.com

SPORT AND LEISURE
Zef Control
Learn to pilot a thrilling three-wheeled sand yacht on Narbonne-Plage's long stretches of breezy sands. Zef Control also rents out catamarans and kayaks and offers sailing training courses for beginners.
Créneau Naturel.
Tel: 0671 04 85 17.
www.zefcontrol.com.
Admission charge.

Serignan-Plage
ACCOMMODATION
Yelloh Village Serignan Plage £
Situated next to a 600m (650yd) stretch of sandy beach between the mouth of the Canal du Midi and Cap d'Agde, this big campsite offers a choice of mobile homes, chalets and bungalows, as well as places to pitch

your own tent. It has six heated pools, including a covered pool for toddlers, and a lagoon pool with water flumes. A spa lifts it a little above the local campsite competitors, and for those who want an all-over tan there is a stretch of naturist beach.

L'Orpelière, Sérignan-Plage; follow signs to Sérignan-Plage from A9 autoroute exit 35 (Béziers Est). Tel: (0467) 32 35 33. www.leserignanplage.com

Sport and leisure
Lou Calamaire

This is the nearest 'furnished beach' to the centre of Béziers, with loungers and umbrellas for hire, two tapas and cocktail bars, a seaside Mediterranean-flavoured restaurant run by a local rugby-playing legend, Jean-Marc Cordier, a resident DJ and live music three times a week in summer.

Plage aménagée Le Calmaire. Tel: (0467) 35 01 16. Open: Jun–Sept 10am–10pm.

Valras-Plage
Eating out
Domaine la Yole £

This restaurant is great for families, with its own farm and kitchen garden which produce many of the ingredients that go into its regional specialities. These include luscious Mediterranean salads and dishes grilled over a wood fire. It also has its own winery, offering wine-tasting meals comprising seven dishes, each accompanied by a different vintage.

Route de Vendres. Tel: (0467) 30 62 93. www.layolewineresort.com

PERPIGNAN AND THE CÔTE VERMEILLE
Le Barcarès
Accommodation
Camping Club Village l'Europe £

This is one of the few *campings* along the Roussillon coast which stays open all year, although the 600m (650yd) strand next to it is a lot more appealing in the summer months, when the site is a whole lot busier and has live entertainment every night. There's a large lagoon-style pool (summer only), and the choice of accommodation includes chalets, mobile homes and tent pitches, each of which has its own shower and WC.

Route de Saint Laurent, Le Barcarès. Tel: (0468) 86 15 36. www.europe-camping.com

Canet-en-Roussillon
Accommodation
Village le Brasilia £

With a swathe of sandy beach and grounds studded with palm trees and greenery, this campsite offers space for self-pitched tents as well as well-appointed cabins and mobile homes with self-catering facilities. It also has swimming pools and watersports on the beach. Perpignan is less than 30 minutes' drive away.

Avenue Anneaux du Roussillion (CR30), Canet-Plage; turn north from Voie de la Mediterrannee at Rond-Point General de Gaulle roundabout on approach to Canet-Plage; signposted. Tel: (0468) 80 23 82. www.brasilia.fr

Collioure
ACCOMMODATION
Hôtel les Templiers ££

Art lovers will be in their element at this family-run hotel – not only are the walls lined with all manner of paintings, but some of France's best-known early 20th-century artists themselves have passed through these doors. The décor of the rooms is equally eclectic. The on-site restaurant is also acclaimed, with an obvious emphasis on fish and shellfish.

12 quai de l'Amirauté.
Tel: (0468) 98 31 10.
www.hotel-templiers.com

Le Mas des Citronniers ££

A lovely converted house set in lush gardens with verandahs and terraces. The rooms, some of which have terraces reached through traditional French windows, are decorated with soft hues and are all en-suite.

22 avenue de la République.

Tel: (0468) 82 04 82.
en.hotel-mas-des-citronniers.com

EATING OUT
Le 5ème Péché ££

Reservations are essential for this tiny restaurant where a Japanese chef blends the freshest catch from the local fishing fleet into a unique fusion of Asian and Catalan flavours.

18 rue de la Fraternité.
Tel: (0468) 98 09 76.
Open: Jul & Aug daily noon–1.45pm & 7.30–9.45pm; Sept–Jun Wed–Sun noon–1.45pm & 7.30–9.45pm.

Perpignan
ACCOMMODATION
Hôtel de la Loge £

Slightly unprepossessing from the outside, inside this 16th-century building is full of courtyards, nooks and crannies, statuary and a grand staircase in the heart of the Old Quarter. The friendly service is in keeping with a family-run business and the same care and attention has been applied to the décor, both in the

common areas and the bedrooms.

1 rue des Fabriques d'en Nabot.
Tel: (0468) 34 41 02.
www.hoteldelaloge.fr

Kyriad Perpignan Centre ££

With only 49 rooms, this is a businesslike city hotel which offers excellent value for money for a short stay. It is right in the centre of Perpignan, with all the historic sights within easy walking distance. Four-person rooms are available for families, and facilities include free wireless Internet access.

8 Boulevard Wilson.
Tel: (0468) 59 25 94.
www.kyriad-perpignan-centre.fr

Hôtel La Fauceille £££

Just outside town is this sophisticated, contemporary-style 4-star hotel with a beautiful swimming pool area and an acclaimed restaurant. Even the standard rooms feel luxurious – flat-screen TVs, silk bedspreads – but there are also three suites with private terraces, one of which has an outdoor

Jacuzzi. There's also a spa offering facials and massage.

860 chemin de la Fauceille.
Tel: (0468) 21 09 10.
www.lafauceille.com

EATING OUT

Le Garriane £

Le Garriane is a great, colourful little spot just a few steps from Perpigan's railway station. The menu is modern French.

15 rue Valette.
Tel: (0468) 67 07 44.
Open: Wed–Fri noon–2pm & 7–9pm, Sat 7–10pm. Closed: Sun–Tue.

La Galinette £££

A Michelin-starred restaurant in an unlikely location where all the neighbouring eating places are decidedly downmarket. Chef Christophe Comes is not a vegetarian, but he is obsessed with the gustatory impact of the region's finest fruit and vegetables: seasonal aubergine varieties, heritage tomatoes, wild strawberries and more.

23 rue Jean Payra.
Tel: (0468) 35 00 90.

Open: Tue–Sat noon–2pm & 7–9pm. Closed: Mon–Sun & mid-Jul–mid-Aug.

Port-Leucate

ACCOMMODATION

Hôtel des 2 Golfs £

Between the harbour and the sea (hence the name), there's nothing outstanding about this place but there's nothing to complain about either. The rooms are clean but simple, and only five of them have air conditioning if that is important to you, but some have harbour views. Good value for either a beach holiday or as a base for exploring the area.

Quai Paurel.
Tel: (0468) 40 99 42.
www.hoteldes2golfs.com

EATING OUT

Biquet Plage ££

Some may find the décor of this beach restaurant, where one eats with one's feet in the sand in summer, a little bizarre, with its ranks of naked mannequins poised ironically beneath a sign that reads

'Nudisme Interdite' ('No Nudism'). However, its seafood is among the best.

Le Grau Chemin du Mouret, Plage de Leucate.
Tel: 0669 05 68 89.
Email: biquetplage@yahoo.com. Open: Jun–Sept noon–2pm & 7–9pm.

SPORT AND LEISURE

Loca-Détente

Motorboats up to 4.7m (15½ft) with a 6HP engine can be rented without a permit from this agency, which also rents more powerful boats to those with the relevant licence, as well as waterski equipment, fishing rods and bicycles (by the day or by the week).

Quai du Paurel, Bassin Sud (opposite the tourist office). Tel: (0468) 40 89 73 & 0608 64 94 50.
www.loca-detente.fr.
Open: Jun–Sept 9am–9pm.

Port-Vendres

EATING OUT

Côte Vermeille ££

Unquestionably the best restaurant in a resort which in summer is not

short of run-of-the-mill offerings. Ultra-fresh seafood is its big strength.
Quai Fanal.
Tel: (0468) 82 05 71.
Open: Tue–Sat noon–2pm & 7–9pm. Closed: Jan & first week in Jul.

Saint-Cyprien
ACCOMMODATION
L'Île de la Lagune £££
This place offers a unique experience as the entire hotel is situated on a private island. All of the bright, spacious rooms have a private terrace as well as the usual mod cons, and there are also apartments to rent, complete with their own kitchen facilities. The restaurant is also highly recommended for local produce served in gourmet style.
Boulevard de l'Almandin 'Les Capellans', 66750 Saint-Cyprien Sud.
Tel: (0468) 21 01 02.
http://en.hotel-ile-lagune.com

Saint-Cyprien-Plage
ACCOMMODATION
Hôtel Mar i Sol £
A functional beachfront hotel, and a good choice for families who are literally going to spend all day on the beach. The restaurant serves a range of Catalan dishes.
Rue Auguste Rodin.
Tel: (0468) 37 31 00.
www.hotelmarisol.com

PYRÉNÉES-ORIENTALES AND CORBIÈRES
Region-wide
SPORT AND LEISURE
Comité Départementale du Tourisme des Pyrénées-Orientales
The Pyrénées-Orientales Tourism Committee organises one-week escorted Pyrenean rambling and spa trips in and around the Conflent valley area, starting at Villefranche-de-Conflent and including the lower slopes of the Pic du Canigou, plus five spa sessions in the renowned thermal waters of Vernet-les-Bains. Transfers to and from Céret, Perpignan and other points in the region can be arranged.
16 avenue des Palmiers, Perpignan.
Tel: (0468) 51 52 70.
www.cdt-66.com

Le Train Jaune
The 'Yellow Train' operates on a scenic rail route through the foothills of the Pyrénées and onward into the high country of the Cerdagne on the Spanish frontier (*see pp90–91 for details of routes and points of interest along the way*).
Gare Villefranche-Vernet-Fouilla.
Tel: (0468) 96 56 62.
www.ter-sncf.com.
Departures: up to six times daily Jun–Sept, see website for times.

Amélie-les-Bains
ACCOMMODATION
Grand Hôtel de la Reine Amélie £
Despite its name, this hotel is looking a little jaded now and could do with a 21st-century facelift, but it fulfills its brief as a decent holiday stay, with swimming pool, clean and comfortable rooms, restaurant, carpark and a children's play area.
32 boulevard de la Petite Provence.
Tel: (0468) 39 04 38.
www.reineamelie.com

Céret

ACCOMMODATION

La Chataigneraie ££

This former *maison de maitre* is now a gorgeous family-run luxury bed-and-breakfast place. With four twin or double rooms and two suites, all within an old stone building and surrounding a swimming pool, it's never going to feel crowded. There are wonderful views, and the bars and restaurants of Céret are within walking distance.
Route de Fonfrede.
Tel: (0468) 87 21 58.
www.ceret.net

Le Mas Trilles £££

A lovely converted 17th-century stone farmhouse surrounded by gardens and with a large pool area. There are three grades of room, from standard to deluxe, but all are decorated in keeping with the rustic style and most have private terraces. There's no restaurant, but the owners are happy to make local recommendations. A wonderful 'get away from it all' kind of place.
Le Pont de Reynes.
Tel: (0468) 87 38 37.
www.le-mas-trilles.com

EATING OUT

Le Chat qui Rit £

Outside the centre of Céret village, 'The Laughing Cat' offers Catalan-influenced cuisine.
La Cabanasse,
Route Amélie.
Tel: (0468) 87 02 22.

Del Bisbe £

This restaurant offers really good-value set menus in attractive surroundings. In summer, the leafy terrace beckons. In cooler weather, there's a cosy indoor dining room. This is a restaurant-with-rooms, offering comfortable and modestly priced accommodation on its upper floor.
4 place Soutine.
Tel: (0468) 87 00 85.
www.hotelvidalceret.com

Corbières

ACCOMMODATION

Auberge Côté Jardin ££

A husband-and-wife team oversees this lovely guesthouse in the Corbières. There are 12 bright and elegant rooms with a slight minimalist feel and a restaurant that is popular with locals as well as guests. There's also a swimming pool in the grounds.
Conilhac-Corbières.
Tel: (0468) 27 08 19. www.
auberge-cotejardin.com

Font-Romeu

ACCOMMODATION

Hôtel Pyrénées £

The 1970s seem to be alive and well in this hotel, but it's a great budget option for exploring the region and, if you can ignore the leather chairs and pine cladding, it offers spectacular views of the mountains. There's also an indoor pool and a sauna.
Place des Pyrénées.
Tel: (0468) 30 01 49. www.
hotel-des-pyrenees.com

Huttopia Font-Romeu £

Wooden chalets which sleep up to six people and have en-suite showers and WCs, kitchens equipped with microwaves and dishwashers and wood-burning stoves. It's all set in a large expanse of wooded land with great views. This well-equipped site is one of the best bases for an active holiday exploring the wide open spaces of the Parc Naturel Régional.

Route de Mont-Louis (N116), Font-Romeu; signposted from all directions. Tel: (0468) 30 09 32. www.huttopia.com

EATING OUT

La Chaumière £

Friendly and affordable small brasserie which specialises in Catalan-influenced dishes and fresh, locally sourced ingredients.

96 avenue Emmanuel Brousse.
Tel: (0468) 30 04 40.
Open: Wed–Sun noon–2pm & 7–9pm. Closed: Mon–Tue, late Jun–mid-Jul & middle two weeks in Oct.

ENTERTAINMENT

Casino Font-Romeu

Font-Romeu is literally the high point of the nightlife scene in this part of the world. During the winter sports season, there's plenty

of *après-ski* activity, and in summer the casino, with its one-armed bandits, roulette and blackjack tables, and its own disco dance club, Le Papagayo, is the resort's after-dark hub.

46 avenue Emmanuel. Tel: (0468) 30 01 11. www. casino-font-romeu.com. Open: nightly 9pm–3am.

Rennes-le-Château

ACCOMMODATION

Château des Ducs de Joyeuse £££

A truly magnificent stay can be found in the striking converted 16th-century castle originally built for the Duke of Narbonne. It retains many of its original features, such as exposed stone walls and heavy wooden doors, while the rest of the décor pays due respect to the history of the place with dark wooden panelling, four-poster beds, plush curtains and medieval scenes depicted on walls. The indoor restaurant is the last word in elegance within the original cellar, while dining outside in the floodlit

courtyard on a summer evening could not offer a more romantic setting.

Allée du Château, Couiza. Tel: (0468) 74 23 50. www. chateau-des-ducs.com

CARCASSONNE AND THE AUDE VALLEY
Alet-les-Bains
ENTERTAINMENT

Casino Alet-les-Bains

Just outside one of the most picturesque villages in the upper Aude valley, the casino looks jarringly modern, but it offers those who like a flutter a choice of gaming tables and slot machines, as well as its own grill-and-barbecue restaurant.

Avenue des Pins, Alet-les-Bains, 32km (20 miles) south of Carcassonne on the D118.
Tel: (0468) 69 91 68. www. omnium-casinos.com. Open: daily 11am–4am. Free shuttle from Carcassonne on request.

Carcassonne
ACCOMMODATION

Campéole La Cité £

Just 3km (under 2 miles) outside Carcassonne is

this pleasant campsite of mobile homes. Facilities include swimming pool, table tennis, volleyball area and more practical offerings such as a laundry area and a bread shop and snack bar. A great family place, allowing children the freedom to roam with the added benefit of a bit of history close by in the form of the city of Carcassonne itself.

Route de Saint-Hilaire, Carcassonne.
Tel: (0468) 25 11 77.
www.campeole.com

Le Terminus £

The original station hotel, dating from the early 20th century, many parts of the Terminus have retained Beaux-Arts features, particularly in the impressive bar and foyer. The rooms have seen better days, but the location is ideal for rail travellers, for those who want to explore the modern Ville Basse (Lower Town) – it's five minutes' walk to Place Carnot where the twice-weekly market is held – and for those wanting to explore the Canal du Midi. The Cité Médiévale is easily reached with the shuttle buses.

2 avenue Maréchal Joffre.
Tel: (0468) 25 25 00.
www.soleilvacances.com

L'Hôtel des Trois Couronnes ££

The hotel itself is modern and rather bland, but the standard rooms have a patio and the deluxe rooms a balcony. The real asset here is the location – directly facing the Cité Médiévale, which is particularly spectacular when floodlit at night. Even better if you book ahead for a room on Bastille Day (14 July) when fireworks light up the sky. Failing that, book a table at the 'panoramic' restaurant.

2 rue des Trois Couronnes.
Tel: (0468) 25 36 10.
www.hotel-destrois couronnes.com

Hotel les Oliviers £££

Les Oliviers is just outside the walls of the Cité. It's a great choice for those on a touring holiday by car, as it is really easy to find (unlike some Carcassonne hotels) and is just off the main N113 highway. It's good for families, too, with 31 self-catering studios equipped with a kitchen nook and sleeping up to five, as well as 29 en-suite rooms which also sleep up to five people.

164 avenue Général Leclerc. Tel: (0468) 26 45 69. www.inter-hotel-carcassonne.fr

Le Domaine d'Auriac ££££

Just outside Carcassonne is this impressive, if slightly dated, 4-star hotel. Its main appeal for many is its 18-hole golf course. There's also a pool and tennis court and two good restaurants with outside tables in summer. This is an ideal choice of hotel if you want to sightsee in urban settings then return to a country retreat at night.

Route de Saint-Hilaire BP554, Carcassonne.
Tel: (0468) 25 72 22. www. domaine-d-auriac.com

Hôtel de la Cité ££££

Right within the old walls of the Cité Médiévale and with its own lush gardens

and a pool, this is one of the best places to stay in the region. The rooms maintain a traditional French style with plush velvet curtains, tapestries and antiques. The restaurant is also highly acclaimed. Driving and parking in the Cité is restricted to residents – the hotel has a car park on the outside, from where there are shuttle buses to your accommodation. Breakfast is included in the room rate.
Place Auguste-Pierre Pont. Tel: (0468) 71 98 71. www.hoteldelacite.com

EATING OUT

Bar Felix £
Classic café-bar-brasserie on Place Carnot, where you can watch the bustle of market day and enjoy a cold drink or lunch. Serves all the brasserie staples, and its easy-to-spot orange umbrellas make it the ideal rendezvous spot.
Place Carnot.
Open: 10am–10pm.

Chez Fred ££
Tucked away from the beaten tourist track, Chez Fred feels a bit like a speakeasy, but behind its unprepossessing exterior is a warm welcome, a menu that is vastly superior to most of the offerings in the Cité, and a pleasant inner courtyard. A local favourite.
31 boulevard Omer-Sarrault. Tel: (0468) 72 02 23. www.chez-fred.fr. Open: Jul–Sept Tue–Fri noon–2pm & 7–10pm, Sat–Mon 7–10pm; Oct–Jun Tue–Fri noon–2pm & 7.30–10pm, Sat & Mon noon–2pm.

Chez Saskia ££
This is the Hôtel de la Cité's less formal brasserie restaurant. The service, menu and wine list, while a little more affordable than La Barbacane's gourmet offerings, all show the same meticulous attention to detail.
Hôtel de la Cité, Place Auguste-Pierre Pont. Tel: (0468) 71 98 71. www.hoteldelacite.com. Open: noon–2pm & 7–10pm.

La Barbacane £££
Prize-winning chef Jérôme Ryon presides over the Hôtel de la Cité's gastronomic restaurant, which is certainly the most elegant place to eat within Carcassonne's medieval ramparts.
Hôtel de la Cité, Place Auguste-Pierre Pont. Tel: (0468) 71 98 71. www.hoteldelacite.com. Open: daily 7pm–10pm.

Le Parc £££
Franck and Céline Putelat's restaurant has Carcassonne's only Michelin star and is priced to match, but worth every penny. Located outside the walls of the Cité Médiévale, this place is still worth the trip for superb and imaginative dishes from the seas, hills and vineyards of Languedoc-Roussillon in stylish, modern surroundings.
80 chemin des Anglais. Tel: (0468) 71 80 80. www.leparcfranck putelat.fr. Open: Tue–Sat noon–2pm & 7–10pm. Closed: Sun, Mon & Jan.

ENTERTAINMENT

Les Jardins de Dame Flore
Continuing Carcassonne's commercialisation (and

fictionalisation) of its medieval past, this 'heritage restaurant' within the Cité Médiévale entertains its guests with non-stop performances by jugglers, fire-eaters and minstrels. The menu is equally faux-medieval.
6 rue Saint-Jean.
Tel: (0468) 77 85 76.
Open: daily 11am–
midnight.

Tournoi de la Chevalerie
If you liked *Robin Hood: Prince of Thieves* (some of which was filmed here), *Braveheart*, *Highlander* and all those other great swashbuckling movies, you'll love this re-enactment of a 12th-century tourney, with knights and men-at-arms clashing with sword, shield and lance.
Les Lices de la Cité.
Performances: end of first week in Jul–end Aug daily 3pm & 4.45 pm.
Admission charge (under 7s free).

SPORT AND LEISURE
Bateaux Solal
Small boat trips along the Canal du Midi from Carcassonne, with multi-lingual narrative.
Promenade du Canal.
Tel: 0607 74 04 57.
Departures: Apr–mid-Jun & mid-Sept–end Oct Tue–Sun 2.30pm & 4.30pm; mid-Jun–mid-Sept daily 10am, 10.30am, 2pm, 3pm, 4pm, 5pm & 6pm.
Closed: Nov–Mar.
Admission charge.

Les Calèches de Carcassonne
Horse-drawn carriage tours around the grassy surrounds of the formidable towers and ramparts of the Cité Médiévale. Departures are from the Porte Narbonnaise, the main entrance to the Cité. Trips last about 20 minutes.
Porte Narbonnaise.
Tel: (0468) 71 54 57. www. carcassonne-caleches.com.
Open: Apr–mid-Nov 10am–6pm. Closed: mid-Nov–end Mar.

Croisières du Midi
The traditional canal barge *Saint Ferréol* sails up and down the Canal du Midi from the quaint canal port at Homps, about 40 minutes' drive east of Carcassonne, passing through locks and under aqueducts and canal bridges. This is one of the most scenic stretches of the canal accessible from Carcassonne. Advance bookings advised.
Capitainerie d'Homps, 35 quai des Tonneliers, Homps.
Tel: (0468) 91 33 00. www. croisieres-du-midi.com.
Departures: Apr–end Oct at least one daily at 2.30pm; Jul & Aug up to four daily 10.45am–4.30pm. Admission charge.

Eau-rizon
Canoeing, canyoning, hydrospeed, white-water rafting, rock climbing, potholing and archery are among the exciting activities offered by this outfit. Equipment is supplied.
51 route Minervoise, Puicheric, 24km (15 miles) east of Carcassonne on the D610. Tel: (0468) 49 99 82. www.eau-rizon.org.
Open: Jun–Sept, with guided canoe trips at 9.30am, 11.30am & 2.30pm (call or visit website for timetables of other activities). Admission charge.

Win'Kart

This 976m (3,202ft) karting circuit is open to everyone over the age of seven, with a choice of mini-karts, 270cc speedsters and two-seaters.
*Route de Bram (D33).
Tel: (0468) 25 67 07.
www.winkart.fr. Open:
Nov–Mar Tue–Sun
2–6pm; Apr–Jun, Sept &
Oct Tue–Sun 2–7pm; Jul
& Aug daily 10am–9pm.
Admission charge.*

Castelnaudary

ACCOMMODATION

Hôtel du Centre et du Lauragais £

A little old-fashioned but conveniently located in the centre of town and with friendly service. There's a good-value restaurant too, serving traditional regional dishes such as *cassoulet*, which is said to have stemmed from this town.
*31 cours de la République.
Tel: (0468) 23 25 95.
www.hotel-centre-lauragais.com*

EATING OUT

Le Tirou ££

A couple of minutes' walk from the Grand Bassin on the Canal du Midi, Le Tirou serves some of the best *cassoulet* in the region, along with other typical dishes and a good local wine list, all in peaceful surroundings.
*90 avenue Monsigneur de Langle.
Tel: (0468) 94 15 95.
www.letirou.com.
Open: Tue–Sun noon–2.30pm & 7–9pm. Closed: last week in Jun, end Dec–late Jan & Mon.*

Lastours

EATING OUT

Le Puits du Trésor ££

Beneath the towers of the ruined castles of Lastours, this gastronomic restaurant has a pretty riverside location and a neoclassical menu which draws on the wild game, fish, fruit and vegetables of the Montagne Noire.
*Route des Châteaux.
Tel: (0468) 77 50 24.
www.lepuitsdutresor.com.
Open: Tue–Sun noon–2pm & 8–9.30pm.*

ENTERTAINMENT

Son et Lumière

Spectacular light-and-music show which tells the story of the castles of Lastours and the Montagne Noire during the dark years of the Albigensian Crusade.
*Belvédère, Les Châteaux de Lastours.
Tel: (0468) 77 56 01.
Email: lastorresdecabaret.overblog.com.
Performances: end of first week in Jul–end of third week in Aug Tue 10.15pm.
Admission charge.*

Limoux

ACCOMMODATION

Grand Hôtel Moderne et Pigeon ££

This building has had various incarnations, starting life as a monastery, but has operated as a hotel for more than 100 years. The bedrooms are stylish and well equipped, and the restaurant offers a variety of menus from its acclaimed chef (*see p184*).
*1 place du Général Leclerc.
Tel: (0468) 31 00 25.
www.grandhotelmoderne pigeon.fr*

Chateau de Villeréglan £££

This is an absolutely fabulous retreat within a

gorgeous little award-winning *village fleuri* ('village in bloom') near Limoux. With only five double rooms and one suite, booking ahead is essential if you want to stay in this baronial manor house. To its 18th-century charm, the owners have added 21st-century amenities including wireless Internet, a swimming pool and a restaurant serving meals made with local organic produce.

1 allée du Parc, Saint-Martin-de-Villeréglan. Tel: (0468) 31 59 43. www.chateaudevilleréglan.com

EATING OUT
Grand Hôtel Moderne et Pigeon ££
In the home of the famous sparkling wine of Limoux, Jean-Luc Desmoineaux tempts and challenges his guests with gastronomic menus that feature adventurous dishes such as *milk shake d'huîtres de Gruissan* (Gruissan oyster milk shake).

1 place du Général Leclerc.

Tel: (0468) 31 00 25. www.grandhotelmoderne pigeon.fr

Minerve
EATING OUT
Relais Chantovent ££
There's a great view from the terrace over the gorge above which the village stands, and a menu that favours local products classically prepared.
Tel: (0468) 91 14 18. www.relaischantovent-minerve.fr. Open: Mon & Thur–Sat noon–2.30pm & 7–9pm, Sun & Tue noon–2.30 pm. Closed: Wed.

Montagne Noire
ACCOMMODATION
La Muse Inn ££
Tucked away in the heart of a hillside village among the thick chestnut forests of the Montagne Noire foothills, this former manor house has been turned by John and Kerry Fanning into a family-run retreat and refuge for creative spirits of all kinds. La Muse hosts writers, painters, poets and mystics for days or weeks, in surroundings that feel inspiringly

remote; in fact, Carcassonne, its airport and its railway station are less than 30 minutes away, so La Muse offers the best of both worlds.
Rue de l'Église, Labastide Esparbairenque. Tel: (0468) 26 33 93. www.lamuseinn.com

SPORT AND LEISURE
Les Lamas de la Montagne Noire
Walk for an hour, a day, a weekend or even longer with a friendly llama to carry your gear along the forest trails of the Montagne Noire. Tailor-made escorted walks of up to a week can be arranged.
Midway between Pradelles and Castans, around 40km (25 miles) north of Carcassonne on the D112. Tel: (0468) 26 60 11. http://lamabalade. free.fr. Open: year-round by arrangement. Admission charge.

Quillan
ACCOMMODATION
Camping Muncipal de la Sapinette £
Chalets are available as well as pitches for tents

and caravans at this site underneath the pine trees on the outskirts of Quillan. All the village's shops and restaurants are within walking distance. There is also a swimming pool with a children's play area.
21 Rue Rene Delpech. Tel: (0468) 20 13 52. www.camping-la-sapinette.com

HAUT-LANGUEDOC
Bout du Pont de l'Arn
EATING OUT
L'Étable à Roussette ££
Excellent grills and other hearty regional dishes are served in summer on the terrace and in winter in the cosy interior of this 17th-century farmhouse.
Les Alberts, Bout du Pont de l'Arn. Tel: (0563) 98 97 33. Open: Wed–Fri & Sun noon–2pm & 7–9pm, Tue noon–2pm, Sat 7– 9pm. Closed: Mon & Christmas–first week in Jan.

Lamalou-les-Bains
ACCOMMODATION
Hôtel l'Arbousier ££
This is a comfortable small hotel with modern rooms and public areas and a leafy, tree-shaded

dining terrace for summer evenings. The restaurant serves reasonably priced dishes based on local *produits du terroir*, with a menu that changes seasonally. The famous hot springs are right on the doorstep.
18 rue Alphonse Daudet. Tel: (0467) 95 63 11. www.arbousierhotel.com

Hôtel Belleville ££
Opened in 1900, the Belleville combines touches of belle-époque elegance with modern facilities, which include a good à la carte restaurant and a less formal brasserie.
1 avenue Charcot. Tel: (0467) 95 57 00. www.hotel-lamalou.com

Hôtel Galimar ££
Small modern hotel-restaurant close to the centre of Lamalou-les-Bains with facilities which include an outdoor pool.
17 boulevard Saint-Michel. Tel: (0467) 95 22 99. www.galimar.fr

ENTERTAINMENT
Le Casino Lamalou-les-Bains
No 19th-century spa resort is complete

without a casino, and Lamalou-les-Bains has its own, within a rather grand belle-époque building on the main square. Roulette, poker and other games of chance are on offer, along with slot machines.
26 avenue Charcot. Tel: (0467) 95 77 54. www.joa-casino.com. Open: 9pm–2pm.

Mazamet
ACCOMMODATION
La Demeure de Flore £££
Just outside Mazamet, this gracious old manor house with eleven bedrooms is an excellent and comfortable place for a couple of nights' stay while exploring this part of Haut-Languedoc.
106 Route Nationale 112, Lacabarède. Tel: (0563) 98 32 32. www.demeuredeflore.com

La Villa de Mazamet £££
Once a private home, this large 19th-century house is now a beautiful bed and breakfast just outside the main town. There are only five guest rooms but they are sumptuous – waffle-cotton bathrobes, polished

wooden floors and tasteful furnishings, all with views of the mountains beyond. There's even a small spa area with a Jacuzzi and sauna, while in the well-laid-out grounds there is a welcoming kidney-shaped pool.

4 rue Pasteur.
Tel: (0563) 97 90 33.
www.villademazamet.com

EATING OUT

Le Chalet du Lac £

Serves traditional regional dishes beside the Lac des Montagnes, where you can swim, sunbathe, hike or fish for trout before or after lunch. Open almost all year round, but really at its best in summer, when you can enjoy alfresco dining on its lakeside terrace.

Lac des Montagnes, 10km (6¼ miles) south of Mazamet on the D118. Tel: (0563) 98 07 26. www.tourisme-mazamet.com. Open: Jun–Sept daily noon–2.30pm & 7–9pm; Oct & Jan–May Thur–Tue noon–2.30pm & 7–9pm. Closed: Nov.

Pizza de l'Arnette £

Specialises in handmade pizza made with organic flour and olive oil, organic wines and fresh-made organic pasta.

3 quai de l'Arnette.
Tel: (0563) 97 01 73.
Email: elodienaumain@yahoo.fr.
Open: Thur–Mon noon–3pm & 7–9pm.

Restaurant Pizzeria le Soleil £

Cheap and cheerful pizza and pasta restaurant on Mazamet's square, where you can watch the Saturday-morning produce market in full swing.

7–9 quai de l'Arnette.
Tel: (0563) 98 03 48.
Open: Tue–Sat noon–2pm & 7–9.30pm, Sun noon–2.30pm.

SPORT AND LEISURE

Ferme Équestre de Castagné

Set in the beautiful hill country of Haut-Languedoc, north of Mazamet, this equestrian centre offers one-hour rides or longer excursions lasting up to six days, as well as personal riding lessons.

La Mole, Pont de l'Arn, near Mazamet.
Tel: (0563) 61 05 58.

Open: daily 10am–sunset.
Admission charge.

Le Golf Club de Mazamet La Barouge

One of the best golf courses in Languedoc-Roussillon, La Barouge deserves to be better known. Laid out by Philip Mackenzie in 1956, it is now a fully mature, wooded course in attractive hillside surroundings, just a few minutes' drive from Mazamet and less than an hour away from Carcassonne. Clubs, carts, caddies and other equipment can be rented.

Pont de l'Arn, near Mazamet. Tel: (0563) 61 06 72. www.golf-mazamet. net. Admission charge.

Lac des Montagnes

This leisure lake, surrounded by woodlands, has 300m (330yds) of sandy beach, 3km (nearly 2 miles) of walking, jogging and fitness trails, a trout-fishing jetty, barbecue and picnic areas, restaurant and snack bar.

10km (6¼ miles) south of Mazamet on the D118. Tel: (0563) 61 27 07. www.tourisme-mazamet.com.

*Open: Jun–Sept daily.
Most services and facilities
closed: Oct–May.
Free admission.*

Piscine de la Lauze

Mazamet's spacious
municipal swim centre
has an indoor heated
pool and a 50m (55yd)
outdoor Olympic pool.
*Chemin de la Lauze.
Tel: (0563) 61 37 16. www.
tourisme-mazamet.com.
Open: Jul & Aug daily
10.30am–1.30pm &
3–7.30pm; Sept–Jun
Mon–Fri 5.30–9pm, Wed
9.30am–1.30pm &
6–9pm, Tue 5.30–8pm,
Sat 2–6pm, Sun 9am–
noon. Admission charge.*

Olargues
ACCOMMODATION
**Domaine de
Rieumégé ££**

If you're looking for a
relaxing getaway in a lush
mountain village setting,
look no further than the
Domaine de Rieumégé.
With two swimming pools
(one is private for those
lodging in the suite
rooms) surrounded by
trees, traditional stone
buildings and cool, crisply
decorated rooms, this is
French country living with

an added touch of style.
Inside and outside dining
offers simple local cuisine.
Half-board is available.
*34390 Olargues.
Tel: (0467) 97 73 99.
Closed: Nov–Feb. www.
domainederieumege.fr*

SPORT AND LEISURE
Aventure 34

Underground,
overground… Aventure
34 offers caving,
canyoning, climbing,
breathtaking *via ferrata*
and *via cordata*
subterranean traverses, or
less adrenalin-inducing
hiking and, in winter,
raquette (snowshoe)
expeditions. All
equipment is provided.
*Mas de Gua, Saint-
Vincent d'Olargues,
2km (1¼ miles) from
Olargues on the D14.
Tel: (0467) 23 27 92
& 0679 35 40 57.
www.aventure34.com.
Open: year-round, call or
visit the website for details
of different activities.*

Roquebrun
SPORT AND LEISURE
Grandeur Naturel Canoe

Two-person canoes and
single kayaks for hire on

the Orb river, with a
range of easy-going
floats and more
demanding fast-flowing
stretches and rapids to
choose from. Lifejackets
and safety equipment
are provided, with shuttle
to and from the start
site and free car parking
in Roquebrun.
*Chemin de Laroque.
Tel: (0467) 89 52 90.
www.canoe france.com*

Saint-Pons-de-
Thomières
SPORT AND LEISURE
Safari Spéléo

Plunge into an
underground world of
strange rock formations
and underground
waterways in these
caverns just outside the
pretty village of Saint-
Pons. A range of
experiences is on offer,
including family trips,
more adventurous
discoveries, and even
underground banquets
with tastings of the best
food and drink of the
region.
*Reservations: Maison du
Tourisme, Saint-Pons-de-
Thomières.
Tel: (0467) 97 06 65.*

Index

Acknowledgements

Thomas Cook Publishing wishes to thank ROBIN GAULDIE, to whom the copyright belongs, for the photographs in this book, except for the following images:

JOHANNE CLYNE 5, 25, 71, 74, 81, 82, 92, 104, 105
DREAMSTIME 13, 17, 19, 150 (SANTAMARADONA); 26 (MASR); 40 (CHRISTIAN_D); 47 (ISAXAR); 59 (CYNOCLUB); 60 (IBSIBS); 61 (BELIZAR); 62, 83 (VANESSAK); 64 (VYSKOCZILOVA); 69 (BALTAS); 73 (ACMPHOTO); 75 (HANSOK); 87 (TELEMACK); 88 (ARENYSAM); 89, 103 (GILLESB83); 118 (MIKE_KIEV); 119 (SERGEYTORONTO); 129 (RALUKATUDOR); 130 (LOFLO69); 131 (DAVIDMARTYN); 132 (PARYS); 133 (CARAMARIA); 147 (LUKYSLUKYS); 153 (BORINOTE); 154 (TYPHOONSKI)
WIKIMEDIA COMMONS 80
WIKIPEDIA / MCA-WIKI 86

For CAMBRIDGE PUBLISHING MANAGEMENT LIMITED:
Project editor: Ed Robinson
Copy editor: Anne McGregor
Typesetter: Paul Queripel
Proofreaders: Penny Isaac & Caroline Hunt
Indexer: Marie Lorimer

SEND YOUR THOUGHTS TO
BOOKS@THOMASCOOK.COM

We're committed to providing the very best up-to-date information in our travel guides and constantly strive to make them as useful as they can be. You can help us to improve future editions by letting us have your feedback. If you've made a wonderful discovery on your travels that we don't already feature, if you'd like to inform us about recent changes to anything that we do include, or if you simply want to let us know your thoughts about this guidebook and how we can make it even better – we'd love to hear from you.

Send us ideas, discoveries and recommendations today and then look out for your valuable input in the next edition of this title.

Emails to the above address, or letters to the traveller guides Series Editor, Thomas Cook Publishing, PO Box 227, Coningsby Road, Peterborough PE3 8SB, UK.

Please don't forget to let us know which title your feedback refers to!